D0952051

The
Catholic
Parish
Today

SUBSTANTIAL, CONTROVERSIAL
AND UNCENSORED

BRIAN T. JOYCE

© 2015, Brian T. Joyce
First Edition
No part of this book may be reproduced or transmitted in any form
or by any means, electronic or mechanical, including photocopying,
recording, or by any information storage and retrieval system
without written permission from both the copyright owner and
the publisher of this book.

Published by Aventine Press
55 E Emerson Street
Chula Vista, CA 91911
www.aventinepress.com

ISBN: 978-1-59330-895-7

Library of Congress Control Number: 2015915754
Library of Congress Cataloging-in-Publication Data
The Catholic Parish Today / Brian T. Joyce

Printed in the United States of America
ALL RIGHTS RESERVED

Acknowledgements

In preparing this book, I received invaluable assistance from four people in particular. Barbara Doan and Marilyn Joost spent many hours providing secretarial support. To Marilyn fell the daunting task of collating and categorizing the many documents contained herein. To both, I am humbly indebted. Copyeditor Alfred J. Garrotto lent his expertise to the project by providing unity of style to a varied collection of homilies, weekly bulletin letters, and articles that span many years. Finally, I can't say enough about the contributions of my personal secretary, Robin Morley, who was there to assist me throughout this project and help bring it to fulfillment. To all four I am deeply grateful.

Table of Contents

FOREWORD

After 52 years as an ordained priest and 35 years as pastor, first at St. Monica's Parish in Moraga for nine years and more recently for 26 years as pastor of Christ the King Parish in Pleasant Hill, I do have some ideas on what works, what doesn't work and what is badly needed in parish life today. This book is my attempt to share these thoughts with others who care. I guess, when asked what the number one need and goal in parish life is, my answer comes first and foremost from the official teaching and priorities of the Second Vatican Council. My hope for every parish is that, most of all, they will be places of warm, welcoming hospitality. After years of experience, I see the basic building blocks must come down to a vibrant, welcoming liturgy, a concern for social justice, and a strong ministry of adult education.

I read in a recent blog that, since we live in a society today in which education is necessary to make a decent living, our parishes and pastors must take into consideration the education and interests of our parishioners. To do this, over the last 26 years, in addition to regular adult education sessions designed to be interesting, well-publicized, and well-attended, I have leaned on three formats: (1) regular letters by the pastor in the weekly bulletin, some of which are reprinted here as helpful models; (2) homilies that include information and challenges for everyone; and (3) finally, and perhaps most uniquely, what has been called a "four-minute special" of adult education after communion.

The "four-minute special" comes from Bishop Ken Untener[1] of Saginaw, Michigan, who stressed adult education and modeled service as roles of bishop or pastor. At his installation as bishop, he introduced himself as, "Ken, I'm your waiter."[2] Bishop Untener also refused to ordain any male priests when he could not ordain women priests as well. He introduced into each and every parish in his diocese what he called the "four-minute special." Shortly after I adopted his idea at Christ the King Parish, I appeared on a panel with Bishop Untener in New York, where he congratulated me on the content of my "specials," and then proceeded to point out that I had actually gone seven seconds over and that was unacceptable! He said it should be like a TV or radio announcement, where you have to be exact about the time with no possibility of going over. I'm sure his warning was and is well-advised. I recently inquired about how it was going in his home diocese after his death and was told that they are still faithfully following his directive. However, one pastor's four-minute special went on for seventeen minutes!

I'm sure you will notice in the following groupings that I have reversed the content of my book to put *Controversial* first, unlike its order in the title of the book. First of all, many readers will want to begin there and go no further; secondly, what may be controversial today, like the wrong-headed approach of many of our bishops toward American nuns, may quickly become old news and irrelevant. Other controversial topics are perennial, like issues around marriage and divorce in the Church, issues around politics and longstanding controversies, for example the practice and celebration of Halloween (is it Christian?).

The second grouping, which I've designated as *Substantial*, consists primarily of letters and "four-minute specials" about the meaning of Vatican II and its impact on today's practice, devotion, and tradition.

The third grouping, now called the *Uncensored* section, consists primarily of homilies by myself and a few others allowing a little more room than usual to continue. Please note that I have carefully considered the advice and wisdom of my predecessor, Msgr. James J. Wade, who repeatedly commented, "No souls were ever saved after ten minutes."

1 *The Practical Prophet: Pastoral Writings of Bishop Ken Untener,* Paulist Press, 2007
2 *My Name is Ken and I Will Be Your Waiter for a Long, Long Time,* Little Books, Diocese of Saginaw, 2014

CONTROVERSIAL . . .

The following group of weekly bulletin letters I describe as *Controversial*. You may want to ask, "Why?" The first ones are obvious. They have to do with the controversy around the Vatican investigation of American Catholic Nuns, which began in 2009. The remaining topics include perennial ones, like the role of marriage and weddings in the Church and the controversies around annulments and politics and science. Plus, I include my personal take on items, such as, the shortage of vocations to the priesthood and religious life. Finally, I address what some people might regard as considerably controversial, namely, the ten most significant Catholics at the close of the 20th century.

American Catholic Nuns (I)

Bulletin Letter — October 18, 2009

What comes to your memory or imagination when you hear the phrase, "American Catholic nuns"? If you've been paying close attention here at Christ the King, Sr. Maureen Viani, intrepid Yankee fan and awesome Religious Ed Director, comes to mind, along with Sr. Joanne Gallagher, our effective pastoral associate, compassionate grief minister and absolute magician with volunteers. If you're of an older generation, like your pastor, it may be Ingrid Bergman (*Bells of St. Mary's*) and Audrey Hepburn (*The Nun's Story*) that you recall. Now, if you haven't been paying attention at all, it could be heavily habited figures, always traveling in two's and mostly teaching children in school rooms; but this would be sadly out of date and inadequate to any generation.

A more faithful picture of "American Catholic nuns" would have to include pioneer sisters who made their way across dangerous and lonely seas from Europe, who also headed West in covered wagons to serve the needs of poor and marginalized of their era. It would include nurses who staffed army camps and navy medical ships during the Civil War and who won the heart of San Franciscans during the '06 Quake and Fire. There would be those who established and directed this country's largest private school system, some of its largest health care corporations and presided over Catholic colleges when "men only" was the standard for all other public and private universities. It would include the post-war explosion of vocations in numbers never approached before or since in the history of religious life. It would count over 350 communities that responded faithfully to the Vatican II directives to update constitutions and conduct to return to the values of their founders and develop ways to apply those values to current times. It would also include the generous response to the Vatican call that each community share 10 percent of its members to serve the poor of Latin America.

In the past four decades, the number of women religious in the U.S. has declined 66 percent from a record high of 180,000 to 59,000, with 90 percent now over the age of 60, and a median age over 70. Only a few hundred are in their 30s. These sisters are still doing considerable "heavy lifting" in parish ministry, religious education, health care, demonstrations for peace and for human life, just immigration, and the well-being of women and dependent children. They continue to witness to Catholic life and values and are unafraid to discuss or listen to issues about which much of the Church leadership remains silent. While traditional habits and convent life are less common, these sisters recently raised seven million dollars to support the work of their colleagues in the aftermath of Katrina. In the last 20 years, at least nine of these sisters suffered violent deaths for peace and justice abroad. In an age of declining Mass attendance, closure of parishes, clergy sex abuse and episcopal cover-ups, "American Catholic nuns" today and yesterday, without claiming perfection, give us something to be thankful for and proud about.

Now, you may find this difficult to believe, especially given a Church with enough public scandals to deal with, but the Vatican has recently decided to launch two separate investigations into the lives and conduct of these women who continue to make us look good! The first is called an "Apostolic Visitation" to "assess the quality of religious life" of the 59,000 women in religious communities in the U.S. A second investigation is underway to look specifically at the LCWR (Leadership Conference of Women Religious), an association of the leadership of 95 percent of religious communities in the U.S., with the stated aim "to assist them to collaborate on behalf of the Gospel." The first assessment about the "quality of religious life" asks questions like, "Are daily Eucharist celebrations according to approved liturgical norms?" and "How does your community deal with sisters who dissent publicly from authoritative teaching?" The second investigation of the LCWR calls for a "doctrinal assessment concerning views on homosexuality, ordination of women, and Jesus as the unique and only way to salvation."

All very strange! Next, I'll explore the why (motivation), the way (process), and the how much (funding) of these studies.

American Catholic Nuns (II)

Bulletin Letter — October 25, 2009

Last weekend I promised an update on the process (the what), motivation (the why) and funding (the how much) of the two Vatican sponsored "investigations" of our American nuns which are currently underway. Process (the what) – Described as a visitation "to evaluate the quality of life" of active (as opposed to cloistered) women religious in the U.S., this first evaluation consists of four phases.

Phase One: An "Apostolic Visitator," Mother Mary Clare Millea, an American nun who lives in Rome and is Superior General of her own Order, has contacted 127 of the Superiors of Women's Orders either one on one, or by phone, either here or in Rome.

Discussions to surface hopes and concerns have run about 50 minutes and have been open and friendly. Included in each conversation has been a request for volunteer sisters to serve on teams for upcoming onsite visitations. Acceptance of this invitation requires the taking of an oath of fidelity and a further oath of complete secrecy.

Phase Two: A thirty-six page questionnaire has been sent to all local superiors to be filled out and returned by mid-November. The questionnaire asks for statistical data, essay style responses to any hopes and concerns, and submission of the Orders' Constitution, a list of property owned and the most recent financial audit.

Interesting questions include: What are the procedures for dealing with civil disobedience and criminal activity? What is the process for responding to sisters who publically dissent from Church teaching, discipline, or Congregational decisions? What recent initiatives have you made to attract new members? Do your sisters participate in the Eucharist according to approved liturgical norms? Do sisters offer reflections in place of homilies by priest or deacon? How does your manner of dress bear witness to your consecration?

Phase Three: A number of communities will be selected for on-site visits, apparently based on their answers to the questionnaire, the interview with Superiors, or anecdotal information received from Bishops or other interested parties.

Phase Four: Mother Mary Clare Millea will compile a report of the "Apostolic Visitation" and submit it to Rome by mid-2011. It will be confidential and its contents and conclusions will not be shared with any of the communities under discussion, nor with their leadership teams nor Major Superiors.

The second "investigation," a doctrinal assessment directed at the Leadership Conference of Women Religious is either more straightforward or more vague. A summer letter from the Vatican raised questions around the issues of ordination of women, homosexuality, and that Jesus is the only way to salvation. The Leadership Conference has had one meeting with the appointed "investigators" (Bishop Leonard Blair of Toledo and Msgr. Charles Brown from the Vatican). They plan to meet in the fall with a response to the concerns expressed.

Motivation (the why) – The announced motivation seems innocent and straightforward. According to Mother Millea, "it is an opportunity for us to reevaluate ourselves, to make our reality known and also to be challenged to live authentically who we say we are." Others point out this is the first time ever that all the congregations of an entire nation have been "investigated." Church historians say an "apostolic visitation" is usually ordered when a particular community has gone seriously astray, like the visitation of American seminaries in the wake of the clergy sex abuse scandal and the current investigation of the Legionnaires of Christ. Still others complain that the reason and the process more clearly resemble a grand jury indictment where there is reasonable suspicion of serious wrongdoing coupled with secret proceedings. Right or wrong, the suspicion remains that all this is a smoke screen to get sisters back in the habit, back in the convent, and back in line.

Funding (how much) – Last summer a Vatican letter to the heads of U.S. congregations suggested that those communities selected for on-site visits pay for the costs of visitation teams. More recently the Vatican projected the cost of the three year study at 1.1 million and asked that U.S. Bishops help offset the expenses. In a July interview, Mother Millea said the U.S. Conference of Bishops would not be funding this effort and "anyone who has contributed has not wanted their name to be publicized."

Finally, here's what I would hope for. First of all, more transparency and less secrecy would be a benefit for all. After all, I can't put a shred of evaluation in an employee's file without the employee having full access to it. Secondly, I trust that the Vatican statements and those of Mother Millea will come true and that this proves to support and enhance the life and work of all our sisters. Thirdly, I hope these two "investigations" become the cause for the Vatican and ourselves to celebrate and give public thanks for the holy and heroic ministry of our sisters. Lastly, what I do not expect or hope for is a huge increase in religious vocations. The amazing increase of vocations in the post-WWII Church is unparalleled in all of Church history. The teaching of Vatican II about the sacredness of marriage and the call for lay vocations to ministry is clearly a success. Then too, the size of Catholic families is no longer as large, at the same time as a broad choice of careers and lay ministry for women has demolished the tradition of "marriage or convent!!" Just ask the countless women doctors, soldiers, CEOs, college presidents and politicians. I think the vocation to religious life remains precious but no longer stands as a solitary choice.

What to do – I have two suggestions: read over the statement of appreciation and support in today's fold-out and consider signing it at one of the tables hosted by our Women of Magdala.

Remember that on the weekend of December 13 there is the annual Religious Retirement collection which goes primarily to communities of women religious in need of elder care and retirement funds.

The Investigation of American Catholic Nuns (III)

Bulletin Letter — May 2, 2010

The "investigation" of our American Catholic nuns (technically called an Apostolic Visitation) is proceeding on schedule. This is true despite widespread criticism and despite the fact that without conversation, planning or collusion of any kind, many religious communities have responded to the detailed 36-page Vatican questionnaire (Phase II) with either very limited minimal responses or by politely submitting their long ago approved constitution and by-laws as answer enough. On-site visits (Phase III), actually nineteen, have been scheduled for April, May and June, with more to come in the fall. One has been completed here in our own diocese with the Mission San Jose Dominicans. The visits are being conducted with graciousness, politeness, and professionalism on all sides. Results will be summarized (Phase IV), sent to Rome, and kept entirely secret from all the participants. Then we wait.

My hope is that Vatican officials will either be so impressed with the record and service of our American nuns, or so embarrassed by the whole procedure that they will either respond with compliments and affirmation or let the process die a quiet and natural death.

My fear is that no matter how positive and supportive the overall results may be, armed with a few slight areas of criticism, those who started the process in the first place will simply follow their own agenda; meanwhile many continue to wonder what exactly was the point of all this to begin with. It may well prove to be to mandate a gradual return to Pre-Vatican II criteria and standards for vowed religious life. The fact that American nuns, more than anyone else, have followed the values and reform of the Council, has exposed them more than anyone else to those who might oppose the Council and its renewal.

As the "investigation" is ongoing, so are the reactions it provokes, which include shock, sadness and a smile.

Shock. The first reaction, certainly from your average Catholic parishioner has to be shock. We know that despite all the "little nuns" cartoons, the funny nun stories, and the occasional memories of a tough nun with the legendary ruler in hand, American Catholics treasure and trust their women religious with fond and more accurate memories and ongoing admiration for their current witness and service. They know that it has been primarily selfless religious who have built the largest private school system in the world's history to educate ourselves and our children. They have produced the largest private healthcare system in the nation to care for the sick and the poor. And they have established social services that range from eldercare, to nursery and the preborn. Over 4,000 signatures by our parishioners to support and defend the sisters after a single announcement witness to the shock registered. Typical reactions include shock that, given the many areas for which the Church might well be embarrassed and could reasonably hope for an "investigation," Vatican officials have chosen the one group that continually makes us look good for a change!

Sadness. When you think of the number of elderly sisters who have given 50, 60 or more years of selfless service to the Church, only to hear they are being "investigated" by the Vatican and challenged by the Church they have faithfully and at times painfully continued to serve, can you imagine how distressed, confused, and betrayed they must feel? I would hope and pray that Vatican officials can imagine as well, and feel the sadness.

Smile. The sisters I talk with, some active, some retired, and some in key leadership posts, have the faith and integrity to smile at it all. They may be being critiqued and criticized by Vatican officials. They may be facing their own aging status, decreasing vocations and dwindling numbers, but they are well aware that in the past they have had to adapt to a foreign land, to a new world, and more recently to the challenges of modern society, and they have done it. In the past they have faced harassment and persecution. Some few founders have been excommunicated (and later canonized) simply by being faithful to the gospel call and they have done it. In varied hardships at great personal cost, they have faced the difficulties of living up to the gospel, and they have done it. They smile and we do too.

Meanwhile a parallel "doctrinal study" of the largest coalition of American women religious (LCWR) has for the moment been suspended. Representatives from the LCWR have attended one meeting in Rome and continue to try to maintain a dialogue. Is anyone listening? Hopefully, yes.

PETITION ON BEHALF OF SISTER MARGARET MARY MCBRIDE

From Bulletin of June 13, 2010

Addressed to:
Bishop Thomas Olmsted, Bishop of Phoenix, Arizona

Copies to:
United States Conference of Catholic Bishops
Sister Margaret Mary McBride

We, baptized Roman Catholics, strongly encourage you, Bishop Thomas Olmsted, to rescind your public declaration of Automatic Excommunication (*latae sententiae*) of Sister Margaret Mary McBride.

We sign, recognizing that Sister Margaret McBride was faced with a situation that involved dealing with both the high risk of death for a seriously ill pregnant mother of four, and the almost certain death of both the infant in the womb and the mother. While Sister participated in the decision which led to the life of the mother and the death of the unborn infant, that decision was taken only with careful consideration, consultation, and good faith. While church law is clear that objective participation in the direct abortion of the unborn is grounds for immediate excommunication (*latae sententiae*), canon law itself speaks of mitigating and even exonerating factors such as: "necessity or grave inconveniences" (c. 1324), and "no one is punished unless the violation is ... seriously imputable by reason of malice or culpability" (c. 1321). While we are in no way expert or experienced in church law, even a brief glance is enough to show us the law expressly intends to reserve excommunication only for actions that are clear cut, obstinate and deliberately chosen and which even include malice, as well as responsibility. This clearly is not such a case.

We urge you, Bishop Thomas Olmsted, to reconsider your actions regarding Sister Margaret Mary McBride and rescind your formal public declaration of automatic excommunication. We are truly praying for you and for all those involved in this most difficult and challenging situation.

American Catholic Nuns (IV)

Bulletin Letter— May 13, 2012

Did you know that the inventor of the first lifesaving incubator was an American Catholic nun? Did you know the cofounder of Alcoholics Anonymous was an American Catholic nun? Did you know that one of the earliest researchers in DNA was an American Catholic Nun? Did you know that, before feminism and women's leadership became popular and politically correct, the only female university and college administrators or hospital executives in the United Sates were American Catholic nuns? Did you know American Catholic nuns nursed soldiers on both sides of the Civil War, as well as victims of the 1906 earthquake and 1916 influenza epidemic? Did you know American Catholic nuns were active in the Civil Rights Movement and in the aftermath of the Katrina Hurricane? If not, or even if you did, you may want to join us on Tuesday, May 29th, as we travel together to the California Museum in Sacramento.

"Women and Spirit: Catholic Sisters in America" has just a few days left before it closes on June 3rd. Sponsored by the LCWR (Leadership Conference of Women Religious), this exhibit has been shown in nine cities across the country, and this will be its last and final showing.

We've chartered a bus for the first 50 parishioners to sign-up to visit "Women and Spirit." Discover the American Catholic Sisters' quiet courage and huge contribution to U.S. history. We will leave on Tuesday, May 29th at 8:45 a.m. and return by 2:45 p.m. At a cost of $26 for bus, museum entrance, and docent-led tour. Contact the Parish Office for reservations as soon as possible.

Speaking of the LCWR, it has been little known or talked about until just recently. But, in the past few weeks, articles and opinion pieces about it have appeared just about everywhere, including *The New York Times*, *The Washington Post*, *The Wall Street Journal*, *The San Francisco Chronicle* and *The Contra Costa Times*. The Leadership Conference of Women Religious which represents 80 percent of the 57,000 Catholic sisters in the United States, was recently "stunned" by an eight-page directive from the Vatican accusing them of "serious doctrinal problems" and "radical feminism"! The Vatican has appointed an Archbishop Delegate and two bishops to oversee and approve the revision of their bylaws, to pre-approve their plans, programs, assemblies and publications, as well as their links and relationship with affiliated organizations (such as Network, the very effective D.C. lobby of Catholic sisters). The appointed delegate is Archbishop J. Peter Sartain of Seattle, Washington.

The Vatican directive also accused the group leaders and directors of focusing too much on poverty and economic injustice, while allegedly keeping "silent" on abortion and same-sex marriage. Several commentators have pointed out that a crucial focus in the inquiry appears to be the fact that many American sisters included in the Conference and in antipoverty and hospital work provided prominent support to the President's health care reform. The sister leaders reaffirmed their opposition to abortion, but also claimed their right to speak on a "moral imperative," like health care, just as the bishops had.

Ethics and (Non)-Excommunication in Phoenix

Bulletin Letter — June 10, 2010

"Phoenix Bishop excommunicates Catholic nun for approving an abortion to save the life of the mother."

This headline, carried in both religious and secular papers, really caught my attention for two reasons. First, because Sr. Margaret Mary McBride is a reverent, responsible and strongly pro-life hospital administrator; and secondly, she's my cousin!

In my view, the headlines claiming that Bishop Olmsted of Phoenix excommunicated Sr. Margaret Mary and the action taken by the bishop are both mistaken. Technically and reasonably, the bishop did not excommunicate anyone. Rather, he publically announced the fact that, by existing Church law, anyone who culpably and deliberately participates in the direct abortion of an unborn child is automatically excommunicated.

The bishops can rightly say, "I didn't do it. You did it yourselves." But also, just as technically and reasonably, excommunication by Church law cannot even occur unless there is malice, culpability, or deliberate sin at the start! Persons liable to excommunication must not only be wrong, but also guilty in their decision making. That, I would submit, never happened. Media: wrong! Bishop: wrong!

Sister Margaret Mary serves on the ethics committee which, along with the patient, made the final decision. The doctor advised his patient, a mother of four, that given a rare and often fatal condition of pulmonary hypertension, another pregnancy was extremely dangerous, and she should have an abortion. She refused. In the hospital, it was decided that not only was hers an extremely aggravated condition, but the unborn child was also dealing with its own pathology. The committee faced the reality that, if action effectively ending the pregnancy was not taken, both mother and child would die.

The hospital issued a statement that it faithfully adheres to the U.S. Bishops' "Ethical and Religious Directives for Health Care Procedures." But in complex cases, where the directives do not explicitly address a clinical situation, the ethics committee is convened "to help patient and caregivers make the most life-affirming decision."

Just so you know how complicated these decisions can get, Catholic teaching both explicitly forbids any direct abortion and also allows for medical treatment that indirectly but certainly effects the death of the unborn child. Common examples would be treatment of ectopic pregnancy or the removal of a cancerous, but childbearing, uterus!

As I understand it, the ethics committee struggled with the decision, contacted an outside professional ethicist who serves for the entire healthcare system, who advised that the lifesaving and life-losing procedure being considered was consistent with Catholic ethics and values. The eleven-member hospital ethics committee, after discussion and consultation, agreed unanimously along with the patient to proceed. Seven months later, the Bishop and his ethics committee would disagree.

My view is that, while professional ethicists and pastoral moralists (myself included) might disagree with their decision, the hospital, it's ethics committee and my cousin acted responsibly and in a thoroughly Catholic, consistent, and pro-life manner and are in no way "eligible" for excommunication.

I understand why the local bishop, however belatedly, would want to make a strong and clear statement that direct abortion is never acceptable in a Catholic hospital, but I'm sure there were at least several more prudent and pastorally wise ways of doing that.

A chief physician at St. Joseph's Hospital has publically described Sr. Margaret Mary as "saintly," as "the moral conscience of the hospital," and has said, "There is no finer defender of life at our hospital." It has been suggested that she simply go to confession and have the excommunication "lifted." If so, I suggest she begin by saying, "Bless me Father, for I have **not** sinned!"

P.S. We Joyces, Sweeneys and McBrides do stick together!

Health Care and Politics

Bulletin Letter — April 25, 2010

Last week, I promised to address the Obama Healthcare Plan (officially known as the "Affordable Care Act") and our Catholic community. I almost wish I hadn't, but here goes. I have no intention of arguing for or against the healthcare plan that is now in place. There are arguments for it and against it from both right and left. Some say it will endanger healthcare with enormous expense and government-controlled bureaucracy. Others criticize it because they would prefer a "single payer" plan or a strong "public option." Still others argue that the present plan does not protect freedom of conscience and leaves taxpayers liable to be funding abortions, which they strongly oppose. While I have my personal opinions, I'll keep them to myself because these are not the issues I want to address here. Now that the plan has been adopted, for those concerns we'll just have to wait and see. My concern here is the public debate and division amid Catholic leadership, with even the claim that one side represents Catholic Faith and the other has publicly denied it.

The U.S. Bishops, through their administrative board, have strongly opposed any support for Obama's healthcare plan. At the same time, a coalition of Catholic nuns, the Catholic Hospital Association (representing Catholic hospitals and Catholic healthcare facilities) and at least one U.S. Bishop have strongly endorsed the plan. Let me be clear (if clarity is possible on such a complicated and complex issue). My formula for voting or political decisions with Catholic values and the "Church's position" remains the same:

1. Ground your values in belief in Jesus, His teaching, and the Scriptures.
2. Get the facts (this is a hard one on healthcare!).

3. Insist that our bishops give us leadership (no silence, like pre-WWII German Bishops).
4. Listen to our bishops' reasoning and not just conclusions or headlines.
5. Make your own best, well-informed decision.

Now the U.S. Bishops have long advocated universal health care and considered health care a basic human right, but argued that the current healthcare bill at present should be opposed. They argued that the bill would extend abortion coverage, allow federal funds to pay for elective abortion, and deny adequate conscience protection. Meanwhile the Catholic Health Association, representing more than 1,200 healthcare providers, urged support of the bill and argued that, while not perfect, it was an excellent start that would bring meaningful coverage at an affordable price to 32 million uninsured, with adequate safeguards around abortion and conscience. It seems there's a disagreement around number 2 of my formula: "Get the facts." Some have elevated the disagreement to the level of a denial of faith! One archbishop has publically called for any nuns who participated in such open dissension from "the Church's teaching on life" to "cease identifying themselves as Catholics."

I continue to look for and hope for our bishops, particularly as a collegial body, to do their homework and advise legislators and voters on value-laden issues. I believe that to be their responsibility, and I believe they have a pretty good track record at it. However since politics is always a combination of the art of the possible and the result of compromise, it's hard to see how political positions in a democracy can ever become official and definitive Church teaching. Plus, in practice, Catholics do often end up paying for all sorts of things with which they morally disagree. It may be the Iraq War, the death penalty, or torture of terror suspects. Abortion remains evil and deplorable. Universal healthcare remains a basic right. Real life remains really complicated! Wouldn't you agree?

The Church as Demonstration

Bulletin Letter — January 13, 2013

I'm sure that, like myself, you have received many holiday cards and greetings. One that I received needs sharing. It was from Paul Wilkes, friend, author, filmmaker, and U.S. Coordinator of the Home of Hope in India. He writes: "A good New Year to you, with measures of peace, determination, patience and boiling anger about this Church of ours." I saw a similarly concerned letter from twenty-three active Catholic parishioners to Archbishop Burnett. In it they say, "Now we are increasingly concerned about the direction in which we see our Church heading. It is apparent that the Catholic Church in the U.S. is suffering from a shortage of native- born priests who are able to adequately minister to the needs of the laity. Consequently, we are extremely disheartened to hear of the hierarchy's opposition to considering possible solutions that could include changes in celibacy requirements and the removal of discrimination between genders, beginning with the opening of the diaconate to qualified women. We recognize there is an increasing population of younger people (sadly, including many of our own children), who do not believe the Church is relevant to life today and no longer attend Mass or receive the Sacraments on a regular basis."

What gives me hope and insight about the Church today is a change in definition from the one I grew up with. Years ago, we thought of the Church as a "perfect society" or as a club you need to belong to in order to be "saved." The impression given was "outside the Church (and faithful attendance) there is no salvation." Recently, after the experience of Vatican II and years of pastoral experience, I think of the Church as more of a demonstration, like those for peace, civil rights and workers' rights. The Church as a demonstration is a necessary instrument for God's gospel and presence in the world and in our lives.

My old friend Fr. Bill O'Donnell was described at his death as "the saint of Berkeley." With more than 200 arrests, he was familiar with public demonstrations and always gave the advice that three things are necessary to be part of a demonstration: 1) that you show up; 2) that you make a friend; and, 3) that you have fun. As our parish mission statement says, the whole point of the Church-as-demonstration is to "hear the gospel and make a difference." But to do that, some of us must be faithful in showing up at least some of the time, making friends and building community, and having enriching fun in terms of our spirituality, our hope, and our joy. Speaking of having fun, I've included a poem that reminds us what God does for us. Of all things it is entitled, "Send in the Clowns."

"Send in the Clowns"

Send in the Clowns,
O Holy One,
what good news it is
that when the wine of abundant life gives out,
you find a way to keep the celebration going.
Just when we are convinced that the worst thing
that can happen is what always happens,
you send bright signs
that the party has just begun.
Just when we are happy to descend into despair,
you send in the clowns
and place party hats atop our frowning faces,
daring us just to try not to smile.
Into this world of wonder,
your beloved Cosmic Celebrant came,
with the last word on the subject—

silencing the political party poopers
and the religious prudes—
pronouncing blessing without end
and no good reason to stop the music.
Hallelujah! Blessed is your name.
Amen

Communion Under the Form of Wine

Bulletin Letter — September 16, 2001

Our Catholic belief is that the person of Jesus Christ becomes really present to us, both through the form of the consecrated bread of communion and also through the form of the consecrated wine. On occasion some Catholics, generally for health reasons, receive only from the wine and avoid the bread of communion. We believe they are receiving Jesus full and entire, just as those who choose only the consecrated bread and bypass the consecrated cup. However Jesus' words at the Last Supper set the standard and remain his invitation, "Take and eat . . . . Take and drink." Here's the question: do you receive both bread and wine, or do you skip the consecrated wine, and if so why?

In the 1970s communion from the cup was introduced with considerable enthusiasm as a proud expression of lay participation in the Mass and a faithful, if long overdue, return to the command of scripture. We offer communion under both forms here at Christ the King at every daily Mass and on weekends at the 5 p.m., 8 a.m. and 10:45 a.m. Masses. We only omit it when the numbers seem consistently overwhelming (9:15 a.m.) and the Eucharistic ministers available (7 a.m. and 12:15 p.m.) seem consistently too few. Many congregations report only a 10-to-20 percent participation as the norm, as parishes that have introduced communion under both forms struggled with fears of germs, bacteria, and even HIV! But according to repeated medical surveys, no one has become sick from consuming the sacrament from the common cup. "The practice has never been found responsible for the spread of infection in the 19 centuries during which it has been used. According to Dr. David Gould, who authored a study on the common cup for the Anglican Church in Canada, there has been some close scrutiny done the past 40 years, looking for just such an instance. Anne LaGrange Loving, a professor of microbiology in New Jersey, completed a 10-week study which shows no difference in illness rates among people who share the cup regularly, those who pass it by, and those who haven't been inside a church in decades!

Here at Christ the King, it appears as if about 25-35 percent received the cup in the front of church, and 10 percent or less in the back. Do so many bypass the chalice out of habit, hurry, convenience, or what? The question remains, "If not, why not?" and Jesus' invitation remains, as we "take and eat . . . take and drink!"

Pope Francis's View of Heaven

Bulletin Letter — June 23, 2013

Here's an article published in the *London Tablet* entitled, "Pope Francis's View of Heaven."

"It is a traditional maxim that, though Catholics are required to believe in hell, they are not required to believe there is anybody in it. They are not required to believe that, despite the doctrine, there is 'no salvation outside the Church,' atheists and people with other varieties of non-Catholic belief will automatically be refused entry at the gates of Heaven. In one sense, therefore, Pope Francis was not saying anything new when he told Vatican employees at their morning Mass that Christ had redeemed the whole of humankind.

"'Even the atheists? Even them,' he said. 'Everyone'—a word that appeared about 20 times in his informal homily. 'The Lord has redeemed all of us, everyone, with the blood of Christ: everyone, not just Catholics. Everyone!'

"In another sense, however, he was treading on controversial ground, for it may seem to be a short step from that to saying that being Catholic does not matter. He did not take that step, of course, but therein lies the heart of an issue that preoccupied his predecessor, Benedict XVI.

"Benedict repeatedly warned that that way led to relativism (the idea that all religions were of equal merit) and syncretism (the idea that all religions were really saying the same thing). Benedict had reined in theologians who he felt had gone too far towards relativism and syncretism.

"In a previous generation, Karl Rahner had promoted the idea that virtuous non-Catholics, whether of other faiths or of none, could be regarded as 'anonymous Christians'— Christians, who did not know they were Christians. By virtue of that assumption, the doctrine 'no salvation outside the Church' could still be true. These 'saved' non-Catholics were implicitly inside the Church even if they did not want to be. But his idea was widely criticized. In a recent Vatican document, it says people outside Christianity are 'in a gravely deficient situation in comparison with those who, in the Church, have the fullness of the means of salvation,' and that non-Catholic Christian communities should be withheld from the status of 'Churches, because they have 'defects.'

"The dismissive tone was in contrast to the far warmer language the Second Vatican Council had adopted in 1965, which said that the Catholic Church 'rejects nothing that is true and holy in these religions,' and added, 'She regards with sincere reverence those ways of conduct and of life, those precepts and teachings which, though differing in many aspects from the ones she holds and sets forth, nonetheless often reflect a ray of that Truth which enlightens all men.' All men—everyone. That seems much closer to the attitude of Pope Francis than of Benedict. Same faith, but a very different tone."

The Church as "Catholic"

Bulletin Letter — July 7, 2013

"I believe in the One, Holy, **Catholic,** and Apostolic Church." That's something we repeat easily and frequently in the Creed, but I doubt if we give it a second thought or have much understanding. For example, when we say we believe in the catholic Church, most people take that to mean the Roman Catholic Church, which it is not. As the *Catholic Catechism* says, the word "catholic" means universal, not Roman Catholic. We consider the Church to be catholic/universal in a double sense. First of all, the Church is catholic because Christ is present and "where there is Christ Jesus, there is the Catholic Church." Secondly, the Church is catholic/universal because it is sent on a mission to the whole human race, even from its very beginning when the only members of the Church were Jewish. It was already on a mission to the whole human race, or universal.

Today, we find the Church to be catholic/universal in a much broader and, I think, real sense. For example, even our East Bay Diocese of Oakland sponsors 15 ethnic centers. Masses are regularly celebrated in more than a dozen languages including Spanish, Portuguese, Polish, Kmhmu, Vietnamese, Indonesian, Cantonese, Mandarin, Korean, and Tagalog.

When St. Paul shocked his listeners with his revolutionary saying that in Christ there is "neither Jew nor Greek, free nor slave, male nor female," he could have had no idea of the ethnic diversity yet to come. When we say that as a Church we are catholic/universal, that does not mean that we erase the ethnic diversity, language, and family traditions or try to blend ourselves into a melting pot with amnesia about our nationalities and rich differences. Rather, we need to be a Church strengthened and enriched by our various backgrounds. This may explain why in the coming weeks we will be encouraging people to look into membership in a local Italian Catholic Federation and also our parish Filipino Society. To belong to either does not demand a particular nationality or ethnic background, but only an interest in friendship, family or relationship with Italian background or Filipino culture.

Belief and Dissent: We Need Both

Bulletin Letter — August 18, 2013

On Friday of this week, we'll come to the end of our Summer Adult Ed Series, "Belief and Dissent: We Need Both." It's been a great series with good attendance and outstanding speakers, but some parishioners have asked me <u>why</u> we need both belief and dissent. As far as I can tell, they have quite deliberately stayed away from the series. I think the answer to their question comes from two outstanding theologians, one modern and one ancient. The modern theologian, Karl Rahner, has often been described as "the greatest theologian of the twentieth century." In commenting on doubts about issues of faith and theology, he once said, "If you've never had doubts at all, that means you've never thought deeply enough about the issues to begin with." The more ancient theologian would be St. Augustine, who in the fourth century when preaching about faith in God said, "If you have understood, it is not God." In other words, if you have figured out who God is, then you are dealing with some lesser reality. It all reminds me of one of my favorite books of the 1960s and my lifetime. I especially appreciated the title, *Your God is Too Small.*

We began with one well-known dissenter, Dorothy Day, a very well-received evening enjoyed by all. Then came my favorite of the series, Michael Krasny of KQED fame, who visited us and talked about his autobiographical *Spiritual Envy: An Agnostic's Quest.* After that, we heard from Catherine and Tobias Wolff, an extremely interesting evening. Last week, it was "Why We Can't Be Atheists," with Kate Doherty and me as presenters. Next Friday, our final evening, will be a biggie. Join us if you possibly can. The speakers will be Brian Swimme and myself. The topic will be "All Time Favorite Dissenters: Galileo and Teihard de Chardin."

Galileo, sometimes described as "father of modern astronomy" and "father of modern physics" and "father of modern science," contributed greatly to the understanding of our universe but came into conflict with the Church and its understanding of creation. Eventually, he was tried by the Inquisition, found "vehemently suspect of heresy," forced to recant, and spent the rest of his life under house arrest. In the long run, we learned that we needed both, the dissenters and the believing Church, and that ultimately both were wrong.

Teilhard de Chardin, French philosopher, Jesuit priest, paleontologist and geologist, helped the Church to fully embrace the place of evolution in understanding of faith and our universe. In the meantime, his Jesuit superiors and the Vatican, thinking his views on Original Sin were contrary to Catholic Doctrine, prohibited his writings from being published during his lifetime. Today, his ideas have been incorporated into the mainstream of Catholic theology.

Brian Swimme and Brian Joyce

The first of our presenters is **Brian Swimme**, fellow parishioner and faculty member of the California Institute of Integral Studies, San Francisco, where he teaches evolutionary cosmology. His published works include *The Universe is a Green Dragon* (Bear and Company, 1984), *The Universe Story* (Harper San Francisco, 1992) written with Thomas Berry, and *The Hidden Heart of the Cosmos* (Orbis, 1996). Brian Swimme is the producer of three-DVD series: *Canticle to the Cosmos, The Earth's Imagination,* and *The Powers of the Universe.* A mathematical cosmologist, his central concerns are the role of the human within the earth community, the cultural implications of the Epic of Evolution, and the role of humanity in the unfolding story of earth and cosmos.

I am the co-presenter. If you want to know more about me, this week's issue of *The Catholic Voice* (August 12) has both my letter (finally published!) and a brief biography on my 50th anniversary as a priest.

Immigration and Politics

Bulletin Letter — September 8, 2013

Last week, *New York Times* published the article, "Catholic Push to Overhaul Immigration Goes to Pews," reported that "Catholic Bishops and priests will push a coordinated message next month at Masses on September 7th & 8th to urge Congress to pass a legislative overhaul which includes a path to citizenship for undocumented immigrants." It specifically mentions the Archdioceses of Chicago, Cincinnati, Los Angeles, and San Antonio.

Even though we strongly support the Immigration Bill, you will not be hearing this message from our pulpit this weekend for two reasons. First of all, our Diocese has not asked us to do so; and second, although sometimes appropriate, politics from the pulpit gets very complicated. There are a few lessons we should learn and keep in mind.

First of all, we must be political. Both our Parish Mission Statement and the last line of President John F. Kennedy's inaugural address remind us of that. "To Hear the Gospel and Make A Difference," we must be willing to take actions, even if they are political. Or as President Kennedy said, "Here on earth God's work must truly be our own." To faithfully follow the gospel demands, we must be willing to walk on two legs. The first leg is often referred to as Charity; for example, our St. Vincent de Paul Society, Monument Crisis Center, and Habitat for Humanity. The second and more demanding leg is often referred to as Justice and requires changing things. More often than not, this requires politics.

We also have Church teaching from scripture and tradition which underlines such things as the dignity of human rights, the welfare of families, and even such things as the importance of unions and collective bargaining.

Even when Church teaching is crystal clear (which is not always true) **there is still a lot of room for honest disagreement about the best steps to be taken.** For example, Church teaching on abortion is very clear, but whether the best political steps are a constitutional amendment, increasing family and child welfare, or picketing abortion clinics leave lots of room for disagreement. Somewhat the same is true when it comes to immigration. There are still prudential judgments that need to be made, such as promises of increased border security or the preference for a piecemeal approach. The same was apparently true after hundreds of very clear pleas from Pope John Paul II for the U.S. to stay out of Iraq. Clear teaching does not necessarily lead to full agreement; and the mandate to love our neighbor, which includes welcoming the stranger, does not necessarily translate directly to public policy.

When it comes to immigration, we have a clear bias. First of all, the Scripture continuously asks us to welcome the stranger and the sojourner. These passages appear in the biblical scene in Genesis and remain prominent throughout the Hebrew Scriptures. They are regularly referenced, not only with regard to widows and orphans, but as vulnerable persons who must be treated with justice and compassion. We are also biased by the fact that, for most of us, our parents or grandparents came here as immigrants, sometimes undocumented.

The responsibility of priests and preachers is to remind us of our responsibility, to give us good information when necessary, and to offer practical ways to take actions. Here at Christ the King, our Social Justice Ministry and our Faith in Action program guide us to practical action. One good example is the immigration vigil on every first Saturday of the month. Another is today's tabling which gives us a simple and easy way to contact our congressman (the exact wording of the petition is in today's fold-out). "Living under Obama Care" is another source of good information. On October 10, there will be a town hall meeting on how President Obama's healthcare plan affects you.

End of Life Issues

Bulletin Letter — October 20, 2013

I was away for ten days in early October and it's great to be back. Sorry I did miss one weekend and some major events. As far as I can tell everything went very well without me. Let me comment briefly on a few of the events that took place in my absence. First of all, on Monday, October 7, there was a presentation on "Mary Magdalene Today and in the Gospel" by Kayleen Asbo. From what I have had heard, her presentation was dynamic, exciting and very worthwhile, but the attendance has been described as "puny." Then on October 10, we had the Town Hall meeting with Congressman Desaulnier and a representative from George Miller's office on California Care and the Affordable Care Act (aka Obamacare). That evening was very well attended, exciting, and most worthwhile. To the surprise of our presenters, who expected primarily parishioners who were just a little curious, there was a large number with excellent questions about their own personal situation. Many were without coverage because of pre-existing conditions, disability, low income or unemployment. By 8:30 that evening, everyone got their questions answered.

I hope by now that you are well aware that our Adult Education presentations are consistently worthwhile and excellent and not to be missed. We have one more coming up this Monday night, "End of Life Issues" with Vitas, the local for-profit Hospice of Walnut Creek. Once again we promise that it will be well done and of great value. Join us in church as we look together at important end of life issues that should concern us all.

It's important for us to know what hospice is and what it isn't, as well as helpful ways to talk about death and helpful ways to connect the dying with family, faith and friends. Issues about extended care, tube feeding, and what the doctor needs to know when it comes to "do not resuscitate" concerns will be thoroughly discussed. Join us if you possibly can. Sooner or later we must all face our "end of life" issues.

For those who want to know, on the weekend that I was not present here, I did go to Mass, although in a different place and different diocese. I would have to say the experience was disappointing. The last time I was at that particular parish was about five years ago and my impression is that attendance has gone down slightly, but I discovered the level of interest and participation was now almost nonexistent. I can well understand why many people don't make it to church as regularly as they once did and why, according to some reports, the single largest religious group in the world today is non practicing Catholics or former Catholics. For me, one of the major teachings of the Second Vatican Council was that the goal to be aimed at, above all else at Mass, is the active, conscious participation of all in attendance. What I experienced was a fairly good and strong musical group singing from the upstairs balcony, but replacing all the people's parts of the Mass with their solos. In addition, the homily was hard to understand but blessedly short, plus a lay member of the congregation spoke to us after communion about the importance of opposing gay marriage, and we received a handout with ten reasons why homosexual marriage is harmful and must be opposed. Please note, I am sending a copy of it to the local Bishop with the comment on the same topic by Pope Francis, who recently said, "Who am I to judge?"

Frankly, as a Church we have recently come off a season of disappointment and discouragement. The question is even raised why any of us would not simply leave the Church, abandon Catholicism, and become nondenominational Christians. So far the most fascinating answer I found comes from one woman who says she could no more leave her Church than she could change her gender, race, or blood type. "Catholicism is my DNA," she says. "It is who I am."

While our religion is far more important than the latest regulation or episcopal letter and cannot be simply identified with Chancery or Vatican, the comments and attitude of Pope Francis are certainly encouraging. Among other things, he reminds us that the Church is the home of all and not a small chapel. It is not about rules and regulations, and everyone must obey their own conscience. It is our challenge and task to help this come alive in the local parish experience. Thank you so much for helping us do that together.

Halloween

Bulletin Letter — October 27, 2013

This weekend we celebrate Halloween with a costumed parade at the Sunday 9:15 Mass, plus a special Halloween liturgy in the gym at that same time.

Halloween is an ancient festival with roots in Celtic pre-Christian times. As with most major and many minor Christian feasts (like Christmas, Easter and May crownings), it was long ago taken over by believing Christians and given new meaning and significance. Linked with All Saints Day (November 1st) and All Souls Day (November 2nd), Halloween is old English for "holy eve" or "eve of the holy days."

It begins a threefold celebration for Catholic Christians to first poke fun at the dark and its demons, then to celebrate our heroes and heroines of faith on their victory in Christ, and finally to remember our lost loved ones and recognize our weakness and need for Christ.

The traditional Christian approach at Halloween has been to dress as demons and devils, witches and goblins, skeletons and grim reapers, so that we can laugh at the powers of darkness, because we know that Jesus is victorious. Then we throw off costumes and masks because like the saints we are called to be new persons in Christ. Modern advertising and merchandizing have popularized a greater variety of costumes to include our heroes and celebrities like athletes, cowboys, Power Rangers, Wonder Woman, Spiderman and their companions. Some modern-day catechists have suggested we mix in the saints, especially martyrs who died violent deaths: for example, St. Thomas Moore with his head tucked under his arm and St. Sebastian with arrows protruding! Somehow I don't think that's going to sell, but we still celebrate that we are part of the "communion of saints," that we are unafraid to talk openly about death, and that we smile at witches and devils who symbolize the evil Christ has overcome.

Garrison Keillor explained why his generation liked Halloween by saying, "We always thought it was better for good people to pretend to be evil, rather than for evil people to pretend to be good."

On Ending the Death Penalty

Bulletin Letter — September 23, 2012

This Tuesday evening, we invite you to a panel "On Ending The Death Penalty," which encourages support of the upcoming Proposition 34. This proposition has been endorsed by the Catholic Bishops of California and will (1) replace the death penalty with life imprisonment without possibility of parole, (2) apply retroactively to those already sentenced to death, and (3) create some savings, a $100 million fund to be distributed to law enforcement agencies. The panel will feature Jeanne Woodford, the former warden at San Quentin, who carried out four of the thirteen executions in California since 1978; Darryl Stallworth, who served as Alameda County Deputy District Attorney for fifteen years; and Ron Ahnen, a family member of a murder victim.

When it comes to political elections, the Church does not and will not engage in partisan politics. We do not endorse or oppose candidates, political parties, or groups of candidates, or take any action that could reasonably be construed as endorsement or opposition. We do not make available the use of church facilities, assets, or members for partisan political purposes. We do not authorize distribution of partisan political materials or biased voter education materials on church property, in church publications, or at church activities. The Church does address the moral and human dimensions of public issues, does share Church teaching on human life, human rights, and justice and peace, and does apply Catholic values to legislation and public issues. When it comes to the death penalty, individual Catholics clearly take different positions, but the Church's official position is clear.

The *Catechism of the Catholic Church* explains that "the traditional teaching of the Church does not exclude recourse to the death penalty, if this is the only possible way of effectively defending human lives against the unjust aggressor. If, however, non-lethal means are sufficient to defend and protect people's safety from the aggressor, authority will limit itself to such means." The test of whether the death penalty can be used is not the gravity of the offense, but whether it is absolutely necessary to protect society. The *Catechism* adds that today "the cases in which the execution of the offender is an absolute necessity are very rare, if not practically non-existent." Pope John II and the US Catholic Bishops have spoken out clearly and strongly against the use of the death penalty. They explained that their opposition to the death penalty is based on more than concern for "what it does to those guilty of horrible crimes, but for what it does to all of us as a society."

"To Hear the Gospel and Make a Difference" continues to be our brief, blunt and easily memorized parish mission statement. You help us to live up to it in so many different ways. You help with the faith formation of our young people, from pre-kindergarten to teenage and Confirmation. In these tough economic times you make a difference through the Job Network Ministry for unemployed and underemployed, Winter Nights for the homeless, and ongoing food drives for the hungry. Your care and concern is especially visible in the Saint Vincent De Paul Ministry at our parish door every weekday. Since January of this year you have made it possible for our volunteers to assist 15,597 individuals from 4,176 families or "cases." These mostly large families come at most once every two months and have been helped with advice, support, groceries, and assistance. What makes this possible is the hard work of our volunteers and your generosity four times a year in a quarterly collection.

Labor Day and Politics

Bulletin Letter — September 2, 2012

For a long time, Labor Day has meant not just a four-day weekend that ends the summer, but a celebration of labor itself, labor unions, and workers. It also signals the beginning of the national political election campaign. Both the Labor Day and the politics have greatly changed.

Labor Day – The United States Conference of Catholic Bishops has just released a Labor Day statement which reminds us, "Millions of Americans suffer from un-employment, under-employment or are living in poverty as their basic needs too often go unmet. This represents a serious economic and moral failure for our Nation." According to the Bishops, the "terrible human costs" of a broken economy include workers being exploited or mistreated, stagnant or falling wages, and stress on families. As a result, "Many employees struggle for just wages, a safe work place, and a voice in the economy, but they cannot purchase the goods they make, stay in the hotels they clean, or eat the foods they harvest, prepare, or serve." The bishops contend, "Every institution in society—businesses, governments, unions and private institutions—should collaborate to create an economy that serves the person rather than the other way around."

Politics - The U.S. Bishops have also issued a statement on politics entitled, "Faithful Citizenship." In it they state, "We do not tell Catholics how to vote. The responsibility to make political choices rests with each person and his or her properly formed conscience." However, I strongly suspect that at least some of the Bishops have crossed the line into partisan politics. Their joint statement calls for a well-formed conscience and the virtue of prudence, which recognizes and respects that we live in a pluralistic society, that politics is often the art of compromise, and that those who agree on similar values may disagree on how best to implement them. Not all bishops seem to get it.

The bishops' public statement asks, "What does the Church say about Catholic social teaching in the public square?" It answers with seven key themes.

1. **The right to life and the dignity of the human person.** Since intrinsic evils that must always be opposed, they list: abortion, euthanasia, human cloning, the destruction of human embryos for research, genocide, torture, unjust war, the use of the death penalty, poverty, racism, and conditions that demean human life. They do not specify or take a position on *how* this is to be done.

2. **Call to family, community and participation.** Here, the bishops present either a dilemma or at least a tension. While they state that the family, based on marriage between a man and a woman, is the fundamental unit of society, they also call for us to shape a society which promotes the well-being of individuals, as well as the common good, once more without the *how*.

3. **Rights and Responsibilities.** Again without stating the *how*, about which individuals and political parties may strongly disagree, they underline the right to life, the right to religious freedom, and the right to access those things required for human decency—food and shelter, education and employment, health care and housing.

4. **Option for the Poor and Vulnerable.** "A moral test for society is how we treat the weakest among us—the unborn, those dealing with disabilities or terminal illness, the poor and marginalized."

5. **Dignity of Work and the Rights of Workers.** "Economic justice calls for decent work at fair, living wages, opportunities for legal status for immigrant workers, and the opportunity for all people to work together for the

common good through their work, ownership, enterprise, investment, participation in unions, and other forms of economic activity."

6. **Solidarity**. "Our Catholic commitment to solidarity requires that we pursue justice, eliminate racism, end human trafficking, protect human rights, seek peace, and avoid the use of force except as a necessary last resort."

7. **Caring for God's Creation**. "Care for the earth is a duty of our Catholic faith." We need to reverence our planet as a precious gift, rather than just a resource for our use.

Again, the issues and goals are clear enough, but the how and the way forward leave plenty of room for disagreement and very partisan politics, both as voters and as Catholics. To differ and disagree with one another does not mean we become enemies. We need to remember that there is also truth to be found in "your error" and error to be found in "my truth."

Happy Labor Day, and good luck with the politics.

Ministry and Hierarchy

Bulletin Letter — August 26, 2012

This weekend we invite you to visit our Ministry Fair / Ministry Connection in the gym after all Masses. There you will find information and volunteer tables representing fifty-five of our parish ministries and outreach. You are welcome to find out about the many activities, groups and ministries that abound in parish life and, if interested, you are encouraged to volunteer for one or more of them yourself.

Speaking of Ministry - I recall talking about the importance of ministry in our lives several years ago. One very active and busy mother came up to me and said that she didn't have time for ministry now, but when the children were raised, she would get involved in ministry. I said, "Wait a minute. You are very much involved in ministry right now." Despite all the publicity and need for parish ministry, almost every one of you is a "minister" as parent, grand-parent, good neighbor, and community servant. That's ministry and that's important; but at different times in our life, we are also invited to parish/ Church ministry as well.

I was personally surprised and impressed at how many of you had comments on my bulletin letter two weeks ago (August 12th) when I asked, "Why do they leave?" Some answered, "because of who's running the Church" and "because of hierarchy."

Speaking of the Hierarchy - As long as we are "in between" Bishops (no news yet on who is coming), let me share with you what I think a bishop is for and about. First of all, a bishop is called to lead us as a center of unity and as a connection to the larger Church (beyond even the Bay Area), to keep us in touch with outreach, tradition, and the universal Church. Recently, Pope Benedict XVI emphasized that bishops need to be holy. And, more authoritatively, the Second Vatican Council described bishops, not as our bosses but as servant leaders. It's good to remind ourselves that, by God's gifts and Baptism, we are *all* called to holiness and to be servant leaders—each and every one of us.

A Good Reason to Stay – Among the emails I received, one asked, "Why am I a Catholic?" I answered with a quote from myself published in 2002: " . . . without Church, one risks more private fantasy and an un-confronted life than real faith. There is a lot of talk about spirituality without religion and being religious without church. However, spirituality is ultimately communitarian. The search for God is not a private search for what is highest for oneself, or even what is ultimate for one's self. Spirituality is about a communal search for the face of God, and one searches communally only within an historical, concrete community." The fact is we need the Church and the Church needs us. May the Church make a real difference in our lives and may we stay, participate, and make a real difference in the life of the Church.

Speaking of Bishops – On Sunday, September 9th, at the Oakland Cathedral of Christ the Light, we are all invited to a symposium honoring our retired bishop, John Cummins. After twenty-five years of being our bishop and servant-leader and having survived two successor bishops already, he well deserves to be honored. A reception follows the symposium and is free to the public, but it will be crowded. The agenda includes presentations by a noted historian, a noted sociologist, and a lay person (from our parish), and a prominent woman religious.

Good News is Coming! - Many of you have enjoyed participating in JustFaith evenings. Many of you have avoided them because the schedule is too demanding. In early September, you will hear about a much shorter and equally exciting series of evenings. We already have close to twenty-five volunteer facilitators. Look forward and stay tuned!

Why People Stay

Bulletin Letter — August 12, 2012

I'm still in the midst of recovery from recent dental surgery, but I want to say thank you for the cards, warm wishes, prayers as well as your patience and understanding. I'm not yet fully up to speed but will be soon. So let's take a look at a particular challenge to parish life in the coming year.

A Year of Faith - Pope Benedict and the Vatican have recently declared the coming year to be a "Year of Faith," with the focus on "the new evangelization." I'm not at all sure what that means, but if it implies exploring our Faith seriously and working at becoming a more warm, welcoming and inviting Church, I'm all for it! The fact that the year is to officially begin on October 11, 2012, the Fiftieth Anniversary of the opening of the Second Vatican Council in 1962, gives us some direction and real hope.

Why Do They Leave? - It is no secret that increasing numbers of baptized Catholics in the U.S. never or rarely attend Sunday Mass. Why do they leave? At least a few bishops and parishes around the country have been asking, and the answers should be instructive for us. Many commented that they didn't seem to be getting anything out of the Mass, especially the homily. As one responded, "I stopped going regularly because the homilies were so empty and whenever the Church wanted to raise money, they dropped the homily and talked money." Under suggestions as to what the Church should do, came: "Make the homilies more relevant"; "Eliminate the extreme conservative haranguing"; "Return to a more consultative and transparent approach"; "I'm looking for more spiritual guidance and a longer sermon"!

Spiritual Nourishment - I'm surprised that most of the reasons given are not the hot button issues like contraception,

gay marriage, or women priests, but something far more basic
and universal and substantial than that: simply the need and
desire to be spiritually nourished.

Another View - Another view maintains that what we really
need is a more orthodox, obedient, and consequently smaller
Church. I would strongly disagree and point out that when the
famous theologian Yves Congar published his history-making
book on *True and False Reform in the Church* (1952), he listed
searching for a smaller, more orthodox Church as an example
of *false* reform.

Loss of Trust – One person surveyed wrote, "I separated my
family from the Catholic Church and turned to another religion
for a while; and then returned, knowing I had the right religion,
but the wrong people running it." Several chose to specify
that they separated themselves from the "hierarchy." Some
mentioned priests being too distant from reality and others
mentioned "pomposity," "distance," "aloofness." (What can I
say? Nobody has said that to Fr. Donie O'Connor or Fr. Aidan
McAleenan!) Admittedly, we must also put into the mix the loss
of confidence and trust in church and organized religion today.
For many years through the 1980s, church (organized religion)
was the most highly-rated institution in confidence in the U.S.,
outranking the military and the Supreme Court. In 2001, for the
first time ever, confidence in organized religion fell below 60
percent. Currently, 56 percent of Protestants express confidence
in religion, compared with 46 percent of Catholics—both have
dipped, but we more than they.

Our Challenge - Here at Christ the King, I hope we
continue to offer quality homilies, excellent Adult Education,
opportunities for spiritual nourishment (like the upcoming
Christ Light weekend, the men's and women's retreats,
centering prayer, bible study, men's fellowship and mornings
of reflection) and to be a parish that is warm, welcoming and
inviting. In this Year of Faith, but really all year long and every

year, I invite you to be part of this with your participation, support, comments and suggestions. It is something we must do and be for each other and look for and demand from our leadership (myself included).

Politics and the Economy

Bulletin Letter — July 22, 2012

Sorry I missed the Fourth of July in Pleasant Hill. I heard you had a great celebration and the photos look terrific. But let me tell you where I was and what I was up to … **CHAUTAUQUA** in Western New York. Once upon a time "Chautauqua" was the biggest summer adult education movement in the U.S., with hundreds of sites all over the country and politicians, including William Jennings Bryan, Teddy Roosevelt, and FDR, and performers like Jenny Lind, addressing millions of attendees. Today there are only two "Chautauquas" left—a non-religious one in Boulder, Colorado, and the original, more religious site in New York. Despite my reputation and being complimented for "not being particularly religious," I chose the New York site. Along with 7,000 others. I spent a very busy week that was entitled, "The Lehrer Report: What Informed Voters Need to Know." Speakers included PBS's *NewsHour* anchor Jim Lehrer, Pew Research Center president Andrew Kohut, G.O.P. and Democratic strategists Whit Ayers and Donna Brazile, political analysts Mark Shields and Michael Gerson. Catholic Sr. Joan Chittister was one of the speakers, as was the Presbyterian editor of the *Christian Century*.

Here are a few interesting items I picked up as the discussion ranged from the Supreme Court decision on healthcare to what matters most to people in this election season. One focus was clearly the increase of polarization in U.S. politics and the loss of the "sensible center." For example, many voters go to their favorite TV commentators not for information but for ammunition. Independents determined who won the last four elections. They voted for President George W. Bush in 2004, for Democrats in the 2006 congressional elections, for President Barack Obama in 2008, and for Republicans in the 2010 congressional elections. The number one concern for voters is the economy, followed by unemployment. Out of eighteen topics surveyed, the so-called "hot button" social issues like abortion, contraception and same sex marriage came in sixteenth, seventeenth, and eighteenth, with foreign policy also less than important to voters. We also had a long morning session on the Higgs Boson scientific discovery ("the God particle") and the role of the common good in our uncommon times.

Speaking of the "common good," your contributions seem to be uncommonly good in these difficult economic times—from Job Networking, frequent food drives, Winter Nights, Social Justice Ministry, and second collections. Your care and concern is especially visible in the St. Vincent de Paul ministry at our parish door every day of the week. Presently we are helping about 23 different families each day, to the tune of $17,000 a month. Last year alone, you assisted 1,500 mostly large families. We anticipate this year's expenses to go to $211,000. What makes this all possible is your generosity four times a year in a quarterly collection.

Speaking of planning ahead here are a few important summer-to-September dates to keep in mind:
- Friday, July 27th, 7:00 p.m. - Movie: *Women & Spirit*
- Saturday, July 28th, 9:30 a.m. - Sew Fest and Appreciation Luncheon
- Friday, August 3rd, 7:30 p.m. - Fr. Dibble: Books and Film!
- Friday, August 10th, 7:30 p.m. - "Mercy Beyond Borders" with Sr. Marilyn Lacey
- Wednesday, August 22nd, 4:00 p.m. - Diocese of Oakland Jubilee Mass at Christ the Light Cathedral
- Saturday/Sunday, August 25th/26th, Parish Ministry Fair
- Sunday, September 9th, 4:00 p.m. - Symposium to honor Bishop John Cummins at Christ the Light Cathedral

Tomorrow, Monday, I have eight hours of dental surgery scheduled, but I hope to be on my feet and back for the above dates.

Pentecost and Women

Bulletin Letter — May 27, 2012

This weekend we celebrate the close of the Easter Season and the powerful Pentecostal presence of the Spirit of God sending us forth throughout the year to "Hear the Gospel and Make a Difference." The work and fruits of the Spirit are visible in the vibrant life, ministries and celebrations of our parish, in the continuing faith that carries us through good times and bad, and in the awesome power and presence of God in nature and the Universe Story, in the goodness of people who have touched our lives, and in the continuing saga and drama of the Church, the Jesus movement which continues to inspire us.

This coming Tuesday over 100 of us will visit the soon-to-close (June 3rd) exhibit on American Catholic Nuns at the California Museum in Sacramento. It gives us an opportunity to pause and give thanks for the work of women religious and religious women who have shaped the Church in America and who continue to be models and inspirations for us all.

You may recall that, in last weekend's bulletin, I reported on the Vatican's "doctrinal assessment" that has targeted the Leadership Conference of Women Religious, which represents 80 percent of the 57,000 American Catholic Sisters. It criticizes them "for focusing too much on poverty and economic injustice while being silent on other crucial issues like abortion." Actually, the eight page "doctrinal assessment" more accurately compliments the LCWR and the Sister's for their work among the poor, before going on with more critical comments. Here are the remarks of a neighboring pastor, Fr. John Kasper (St. Perpetua, Lafayette), which he recently shared with his parish:

The controversy surrounding the Vatican's issuing a "doctrinal assessment" of the Leadership Conference of Women Religious (LCWR) continues with strong editorials, written mostly in defense of the ministry and influence of Catholic Sisters in our country (http://www.nytimes.com/2012/04/29/   opinion/sunday/dowd-bishops-play-church-queens-as-pawns.html). As Catholics we ought to be informed about the critical issues facing our Church. The Leadership Conference of Women Religious has 1,500 members. These are women in leadership positions of their religious orders, such as provincials, presidents and members of leadership teams. The organization represents the vast majority (about 80+%) of the country's 57,000 nuns. You can access the Vatican's statement at http://www.usccb.org/loader.cfm?csModule= security/getfile&pageid=55544.

You will find it helpful to go directly to the LCWR website (https://lcwr.org). There you can read for yourself some of the documents which the Vatican deems problematic—the major addresses delivered at the LCWR national meetings and organizational material, such as a "Handbook for Systems Thinking." Decide for yourself whether or not the ideas being shared are problematic. Those of you who work in business and organization fields may find it reassuring that a group in the Catholic Church actually shares your interest in good management and effective organization. Systems thinking prevents a group from unconsciously employing the same mental models which are causing the problems that need to be solved. That sounds like an approach which all institutions, including the Church, would be wise to employ.

I believe that one of the struggles in the current controversy is the reluctance, even fear, on the part of a male hierarchy to open itself to the voice and experience of women. The age of the "local priest" being the only academically educated person in the village is long gone. The bishops need to humbly acknowledge and hear the voice of the Spirit speaking from sources other than themselves. There's a good reason the image of "Holy Wisdom," a divine attribute in the scriptures, is a feminine noun – Sophia. The Book of Proverbs (7:4) wisely says: 'Say to Wisdom: You are my sister!' I learned that lesson early on, growing up in a matriarchy—a household with a strong mother, three intelligent and capable sisters...and no brothers. Just my dad and I learning to live with, dialogue with and appreciate the women in our lives. May our bishops soon learn to do the same!

Father John Kasper, OSFS

Presently vigils not of protest but of recognition and support for the Sisters' work are sprouting up principally at cathedrals around the country. For example in New York, Boston, Chicago, Seattle, and weekly in San Francisco. This Tuesday night, there will be one such vigil at our own Oakland Cathedral beginning at 6 p.m. Participants are invited to bring signs, pictures, or the name of their favorite Catholic Sister to demonstrate support and affection.

Pentecost and a New Pope

Bulletin Letter — May 20, 2012

Next weekend, we bring the Easter Season to a close with the Feast of Pentecost (no more dousing!). HELP US BY WEARING RED, a sign and symbol of the fiery love of God's Spirit! Fr. Tony McGuire, pastor at St. Matthew's Parish (San Mateo) and a long-time friend and co-member of my priest support group for over 30 years, recently wrote a fascinating letter to his parishioners. I reprint it here:

> Lately, I saw a delightful movie entitled, "We Have a Pope." It is a light-hearted Italian farce about a man who is elected Pope and, at the moment of the announcement to the world, he has a panic attack and runs away. The movie follows his exploits, as well as the activities of the cardinals, who according to Canon Law, cannot leave the Vatican until the Pope is elected and UNTIL HIS NAME IS ANNOUNCED.
>
> I was struck by one thing in the movie, and it has been an ongoing impression every time I see the cardinals line up in preparation for a conclave or another papal event. What strikes me is how odd this group is: all men, almost all over 70. It seems like such a narrow pool, not only for the major gatherings but for the whole Vatican apparatus.
>
> My fantasy is that, if I were Pope for a year, I would add an equal number of women cardinals to the College of Cardinals, as there presently are men. I would search for mature Catholic women, who have persevered

in the life of the church and have demonstrated clear leadership. I would favor married women and women of all ages beyond 21, a good mix from all parts of the world and of different ideological backgrounds. (As far as I know, cardinals do not have to be ordained. Most have been but there have been exceptions. Anyway, I am the Pope.) The point is that the two groups would begin a process of dialogue about greater inclusion of women in the decision-making processes of the church and the ongoing life of the church.

Scripture scholars are pointing out that there were many women around Jesus who were given significant roles in His time. (I recently read the book: *Jesus, An Historical Approximation*, in which the author, Jose A. Pagola, dedicates a whole chapter to the inclusion of women in Jesus' ministry.)

Who knows what would come of such a dialogue? For sure, it would head off these frontal attacks by Vatican septuagenarians against women religious. They keep repeating themselves and have proved embarrassing for many Catholics. A recent opinion piece in the *San Francisco Chronicle* characterized it as bullying. I agree with that appraisal. At the same time that the Vatican is bullying the Sisters, their leaders are conducting an ongoing dialogue with the schismatic followers of Archbishop Lefevre. It seems to be going the way two equal partners in dialogue operate, with respect, with an effort at understanding, and with prayer to get over the hurdles.

This addition of women in places of authority seems like an impossible idea. But I recently heard a prayer written by Sir Francis Drake, who, in the sixteenth century, circumnavigated the earth. After arriving back at the English court, to the dismay of many who thought he had fallen off the face of the earth, he wrote this prayer, which could apply to our thinking today:

Disturb us, O Lord
when we are too well pleased with ourselves,
when our dreams come true because
we dreamed too little.

Disturb us, Lord,
when we arrived safely because
we rode too close to the shore.

Disturb us, Lord,
when with the abundance of things we possess,
we have lost our thirst for the waters of life.

Disturb us, Lord,
when, having fallen in love with life,
we have ceased to dream of eternity and,
when, in our efforts to build a new earth,
we have allowed our vision of heaven to recede.

Disturb us, Lord,
to dare more boldly, to venture on wider seas,
where storms show your majesty;
where, losing sight of land we shall find the stars."
Amen

Descended into Hell

Bulletin Letter — February 12, 2012

"He descended into Hell!" Would you believe that? For us older Catholic "senior citizens," it is an easy, well-remembered part of the Apostle's Creed we all grew up with. We repeat it at Sunday Mass, barely giving it a second thought. But for many, if not most, it comes as a shock or at least a puzzlement.

Here is the *traditional* and, for many of us, familiar explanation and understanding. Scripture called the abode of the dead, to which the deceased Christ went down, "hell"— *Sheol* in Hebrew or *Hades* in Greek—not because it was the place of the damned, but because those who were there were still deprived of the vision of God. Jesus did not descend into hell to destroy the hell of damnation, but to free the just who had gone before him and were left waiting for him.

The frequent New Testament affirmations that Jesus was "raised from the dead" presuppose that the crucified one was at least visible in the realm of the dead prior to his resurrection. This was the first meaning, given in the apostolic preaching of Christ's descent into hell: that Jesus, like all men and women, experienced death and his soul joined the others in the realm of the dead. But he descended there as Savior, proclaiming the Good News to the spirits imprisoned there.

Or, as the Bible simply puts it, "the gospel was proclaimed even to the dead." All that is well and good, but when we "pray" it each Sunday it inevitably raises the question about how we understand "hell" and what we believe and pray about Jesus.

About Hell – During his weekly address to the general audience of 8,500 people at the Vatican on July 28, 1999, Pope John Paul II rejected the reality of a physical, literal hell as a place of eternal fire and torment. Rather, the pope said, hell is separation, even in this life, from joyful communion with God. Pope John Paul II noted that the scriptural references to hell and the images portrayed by Scripture are only symbolic and figurative of "the complete frustration and emptiness of life without God." He added, "Rather than a physical place, hell is the state of those who freely and definitively separate themselves from God, the source of all life and joy." He said that hell is "a condition resulting from attitudes and actions which people adopt in this life." The Pope said eternal damnation is "not God's work but is actually our own doing." On the other hand, heaven is neither "an abstraction nor a place in the clouds, but a living, personal relationship of union with the Holy Trinity."

Such a statement on hell is strikingly similar to that made by Billy Graham several years ago, "The only thing I could say for sure is that hell means separation from God. We are separated from his light, from his fellowship. That is going to be hell. When it comes to a literal fire, I don't preach it because I'm not sure about it. When the Scripture uses fire concerning hell, that is possibly an illustration of how terrible it's going to be, not fire but something worse, a thirst for God that cannot be quenched."

About Jesus – To me, the key thoughts and prayers I have as we pray the Creed are about Jesus and to tell the truth I love the phrase, "he descended into hell," because I know again and again that we end up not in a future place of damnation but in a present place of desperation and despair, which can well be described as "hell." What a comfort and reassurance it is to say and pray and believe that Jesus has "been there and done that."

A message of hope - As troubled as life is or has been, Jesus is risen, risen indeed, and that is our hope.

Change and Hope

Bulletin Letter — March 4, 2012

We continue to celebrate the 50th anniversary of one of the most important events in the life and history of the Catholic Church—the Second Vatican Council (1962-1965). It was first announced in 1959, by Pope John XXIII and, after three years of feverish preparation (and non-preparation by those who preferred that it be delayed or even cancelled), it opened solemnly on October 11, 1962, with close to 2,600 bishops in attendance.

Even today some conservative and reactionary voices downplay Vatican II and suggest that it did not represent any major change (!), but only continuity and same old, same old. While Pope John's opening and keynote address did not capture or reveal how incredibly far-reaching the Council would lead the Church. It did contain several striking indications and telling remarks that this would not be business as usual. Along the way, he called for Church and Council to proceed without fear, to stress hope rather than gloom, to be alert to modern changes and conditions, to distinguish between unchanging teaching and quite changeable ways of presentation, and to do something about Christian unity rather than Catholic defensiveness. The fact that we don't find these remarks so amazing testifies to how much we have changed and how far we have come in just 50 years.

Proceed without fear - "Illuminated by the light of this Council, the Church, we confidently trust, will become greater in spiritual riches and gaining the strength of new energies and will look to the future without fear. In fact, by bringing itself up to date where required and by the wise organization of mutual cooperation, the Church will make men, families, and peoples really turn their minds to God."

Hope rather than gloom – "In the daily exercise of our pastoral office, we sometimes have to listen, much to our regret, to voices of persons who, though burning with zeal, are not endowed with too much sense. In these modern times they can see nothing but ruin. They say that our era, in comparison with past eras, is getting worse, and they behave as though they had learned nothing from history, which is nonetheless, the teacher of life.

"We feel we must disagree with those prophets of gloom, who are always forecasting disaster, as though the end of the world were at hand.

"In the present order of things, Divine Providence is leading us to a new order of human relations which, by men's own efforts and even beyond their very expectations, are directed toward the fulfillment of God's superior and inscrutable designs. And everything, even human differences, leads to the greater good of the Church."

Modern changes – "At the same time we must look to the present, to the new conditions and new forms of life introduced into the modern world, which have opened new avenues to the Catholic apostolate. Our duty is not only to guard this precious treasure, as if we were concerned only with antiquity, but to dedicate ourselves with an earnest will and without fear to that work which our era demands of us, pursuing thus the path which the Church has followed for twenty centuries."

Unchanging teaching and changeable presentation – "The substance of the ancient doctrine of the deposit of faith is one thing, and the way in which it is presented is another. The Church has always opposed errors. Frequently she has condemned them with the greatest severity. Nowadays however, the Church prefers to make use of the medicine of mercy rather than that of severity. She considers that she meets the needs of the present day by demonstrating the validity of her teaching rather than by condemnations."

Christian unity – "Unfortunately, the entire Christian family has not yet fully attained this visible unity in truth. The Catholic Church, therefore, considers it her duty to work actively so that there may be fulfilled the great mystery of that unity, which Jesus Christ invoked with fervent prayer from His heavenly Father on the eve of His sacrifice. The unity of Catholics among themselves, must always be kept exemplary and most firm; the unity of prayers and ardent desires with which those Christians separated from this Apostolic See aspire to be united with us; and the unity in esteem and respect for the Catholic Church which animates those who follow non-Christian religions."

Good stuff! Even today, 50 years later.

The Church and Holy Days

Bulletin Letter — December 30, 2012

This weekend we celebrate the Feast of the Holy Family. We celebrate family in many ways and in many senses. First of all, the family of Jesus, Mary and Joseph are the source of our hope and source of God's presence. We celebrate also the families of our parish. We pray for them and boast about them, because they are so good. We celebrate and pray for broken and hurting, families that they may find welcome, support, and strength. And we pray for the family that is our Church, which is struggling more than ever these days.

Recently a dying Cardinal, Carlo Martini, retired Archbishop of Milan and once very promising and likely candidate to be Pope, spoke of the Church as badly in need of reform and being clearly at least 200 years out of date. Robert Mickens, journalist and Rome-based correspondent, has described the Church as imploding under secretive processes and medieval structures. Decline in numbers, criticism of leadership, and closing of parishes indicate that our family, the Church, is in deep trouble. Not just a few but many seem to disagree with our bishops on a range of issues from communion for remarried Catholics to political candidates, same sex marriages, and ordination of women. What I notice most frequently is that the criticism of the Church is about "them," whether "them" is hierarchy, clerical leadership, or the Vatican. What we need to remember and recover is that the Church is *us* and we are family.

A recent statement from a newly formed association of U.S. Catholic priests, one voice among six national priest associations (Australia, Austria, England, Germany, Ireland and the United States) was issued by over 360 priests from 148 dioceses and Religious Orders. It calls for our family the Church to remain energized by the vision of Blessed John XXIII who said: "Throw open the windows of the Church so that we can see out and the people can see in." Among other things, it recommends a culture of consultation, transparency, and decentralization at every level, including the appointment of leaders; an end to secretive processes, where active and loyal members of the Church are perceived as dissidents; and the reevaluation of Catholic sexual teaching and pastoral practice.

Despite the disagreements and division, don't forget that we are a family "Called to Hear the Gospel and Make a Difference." From hospital care to university systems, education and Catholic Charities to local outreach and hands-on help, the Church continues to make a difference in peoples' lives that is amazing and enormous. Even in the face of criticism from the Vatican, women religious and sisters we have known continue to serve the poor and help the needy in amazing ways. Our own parish community is raising a generation of young people who are our hope and our future. Just before Christmas they provided over 400 toys for children in the San Francisco Tenderloin and a huge number of boxes of food for needy, as well as our 8th Graders delivering boxes of food to the hungry in our own neighborhood. Be sure to check out the photos of the San Francisco Police Department visiting our campus and being greeted with hundreds of toys for the Tenderloin. We are a family and Church to be proud of.

"Holy Days" and "Obligation" – Technically, New Year's Day is a "Holy Day of Obligation," a phrase I personally dislike and avoid, because it evokes the idea of "mortal sin" and "guilt" and conveys an image of a God easily upset, angry and unforgiving. I prefer to say, "Holy Day of Opportunity," which invites us when we can to celebrate the beginning of a New Year and major feasts throughout the year. It also reminds us that our God is understanding when we have prior commitments, not so easily upset, and willing to settle for our "just doing the best we can do." Join us if you can.

Catholics and Politicians

Bulletin Letter — January 20, 2013

This weekend, our nation celebrates the inauguration of our President, Barack Obama. Here is exactly where and how pastors get into trouble. You will recall our Christmas tree this year was covered with blue lights. At Christmas morning Mass, one woman came up to me immediately after Mass and asked why the lights were blue, and I jokingly replied, "Well it was a boy and He was a Democrat." Not everyone appreciated my humor. Prior to the November election, a London magazine raised the same issue with a column entitled, "Fantasy Politics."

How would Jesus vote in the U.S. presidential elections? According to human rights expert Conor Gearty, he is definitely a Democrat. Gearty, professor of human rights law at the London School of Economics, said in a debate on the topic in London this week that there was scriptural evidence for Jesus' left-wing credentials.

Political commentator James Boys, senior research fellow at King's College, London, claimed Jesus for the Republicans, observing that the Holy Family had chosen to stay in a stable rather than claim housing benefits from the state. Jesus himself, Mr. Boys argues, was a non-union, self-employed carpenter.

But Giles Fraser, former canon chancellor at St. Paul's Cathedral, won the debate after persuading the audience that Jesus would have abstained. He argues that Jesus was too radical for mainstream politics and that, as "an unmarried community organizer," he would have struggled to enter America at all. "He's an alien with no means of support and He's from the Middle East, traveling on a plane with 12 other men from the Middle East," he said.

In this year's 113th Congress, there's a historic high 163 Catholics in Congress as the largest religious denomination represented. This Congress has the highest number of Catholics and the first Buddhist in the Senate and the first Hindu to serve in either chamber. In the recent election a significant number of bishops seemed to tell Catholics how to vote and particularly urged them to vote against President Obama!

It seems to me there are a significant number of issues for Catholics to be strongly concerned about. For example:

- That we protect the weakest in our midst.
- That we turn against violence as a solution to fundamental problems.
- That we look at a comprehensive immigration reform.
- That we help families and children overcome poverty.
- That we call for comprehensive health care as a right for all.
- That we advocate decent work and fair living wages and adequate assistance for the vulnerable in our nation.
- That we call for moral limits on the use of military force.
- And, that we seek to pursue the common good rather than private individual agenda.

However, the question is never *whether* we should pursue these goals, but *how* we should pursue them. We will find Catholics differing strongly along partisan, political and personal lines.

My answer to how we pursue politics as faithful Catholics is always the same:

1. Get the facts and do your homework.
2. Listen seriously to our bishops (however wrong-headed and mistaken some have been in the past).
3. Listen and weigh their arguments and reasoning.
4. Make the best judgment you can.

A New Pope

Bulletin Letter — March 3, 2013

It is an exciting time for the Universal Church as we look forward to the choice of a new Pope. There have been a variety of comments, op-eds, and responses ranging from faith and hope to depression and humor. On the positive side, I've read about "the humble Pope," "The Pope can enhance His legacy," and "the audacity of the Pope." On the less-than-positive side, I've read, "Farewell to An Uninspiring Pope," by John Philip Shanley, "New Pope? I've Given Up Hope" by Gary Wills, and "The Best Choice for Pope? A Nun" by E.J. Donne.

For Catholics, it is a time for hope and high expectations. My own hopes are moderated by the fact that almost all of the Cardinals voting have been appointed either by John Paul II or Benedict XVI, who by and large demanded conservative credentials. What fuels my hope is the understanding that the Church is not the Pope. The Church is the people of God, experienced first and foremost in parish life and ministry. A quotation from Fr. Jerry Kennedy, who died suddenly and very recently, also gives me hope: "My thought these days: Silence, secrecy, and fear have stripped our bishops of credibility and wrapped them in the vestment of irrelevance. Rome has much work to do, but has turned down the wrong blind alley to nowhere. But the Holy Spirit will figure something out!"

This afternoon at 3:00 p.m. you are all invited to "All Are One: An Interfaith Concert." It will be right here in our own Church and will include St. Mark's Lutheran Choir, song and dance by Chorus of Sufism Reoriented, the New Way Team, our own youth band of Christ the King, Dances of Universal Peace, Baha'i singers, and guest soloists. The Interfaith Council of Contra Costa County invites you to join us for a great concert (a free-will offering in support of its work is encouraged) and refreshments will follow in the vestibule.

My Anniversary

Bulletin Letter — April 14, 2013

This week I join you in celebrating a couple of major anniversaries which actually occurred on March 17th. But in reverence, devotion and avoidance of St. Patrick's Day, we're marking the celebration this weekend. It is a **Silver Jubilee and a Golden Jubilee.** As of this year, I have been here as pastor for 25 years (March 17, 1988), and I also celebrate my 50 years of being an ordained priest (March 17, 1963).

Last weekend I shared with you how the last 50 years have represented a new vision of Church. This weekend I want to focus more on the new vision of what it means to be a priest.

In 1963, I was ordained after 12 years of seminary work with all the answers! Six years of theology from Latin textbooks gave me a clear view of who I was and what I was to do. Obviously, I had not figured on the Second Vatican Council. I looked forward eagerly to its "Decree on the Ministry and Life of Priests" (published in 1965). The first clue that should have alerted me to enormous change was in the first footnote, which referred the reader for a complete teaching on the priesthood to Vatican II's document on "Sacred Liturgy," its document on the "Church," and its document on the "Church in the Modern World." For all my preparation, confidence and competence, the following line in the first paragraph blew me away: "Now, the pastoral and human circumstances of the priesthood have in many instances been *completely changed.*"

Classmates like Fr. Danielson are always eager to point out that I was a conservative seminarian and a very slow learner as a parish priest, but looking back, it is absolutely clear that the job description of parish priests changed radically and enormously. If I look at my job description in 1963 as Associate Pastor at St. Lawrence O'Toole Parish in Oakland, it's pretty clear that it came down to celebrating the Mass, offering the Sacraments, always in a solo manner. By 1965, as Associate Pastor at St. Augustine's in North Oakland, my job description had changed radically.

First of all, *liturgy* was no longer solo, but now had to be done in collaboration with many other ministers and a lot of persuasion as we introduced English for the first time in hundreds of years and also encouraged the congregation in participation and song.

The second item of my job description became *ecumenism*, with interfaith meetings and "living room dialogues." That was obviously a great change for someone who grew up across the street from a Presbyterian church and never once in 30 years dared to enter it.

The third part of the job description obviously had to be *adult education*, which ranged from Christian Family Movement discussion groups to Bible Study and explanation and introduction of collegial structures, such as parish council, priest senate, and priest personnel board.

A fourth part of the job description focused not on cult, but on *social justice*. In fact, with a team of Protestant ministers, we bought a building in West Oakland and started the North Oakland Christian Parish, which continues today as more of a food pantry than the catalyst for protest and change that it was originally.

All this leads me to ask, how has my understanding of priesthood and job description changed over my last 25 years here at Christ the King? Liturgy continues to be a major focus, but now with mature co-ministers like the environment committee, the worship coordinating committee, the liturgy planning committee, and our sacristans, with collaboration all along the way. Ecumenism is not the hot topic it once was. But, development of **lay leadership** continues to be a priority, as do **adult education** and **social justice**.

Here at Christ the King, I continue to learn from you and do my best to serve you. Thank you for guaranteeing that the Church and the priesthood is alive and well and that, whatever the future holds and whatever challenges develop in the years to come, we can be sure of the presence of the Holy Spirit, and that She will surprise us and She will figure things out.

Our New Bishop

Bulletin Letter — May 12, 2013

Happy Mother's Day and God's blessings to all the mothers in our Parish and the grandmothers and mother figures, as well.

On last Friday, May 3rd, the Diocese of Oakland received a new bishop, the fifth in its history. He is Fr. Michael Barber, a Jesuit, who will be ordained and installed as bishop on Saturday, May 25th.

Last week I spent three days at a class reunion. There were eighteen of us: ten active priests from an original twenty-two, along with several former priests and their wives and at least one retired bishop. Of those present, all are retired except four. Still active are a family therapist, a CPA, a courier, and one pastor (hey, that must be me!). The overall reaction to the appointment of Fr. Michael Barber was that he is largely unknown. The most interesting and hopeful comment was from Bishop Daniel Walsh, who had served for eleven years as the Bishop of Santa Rosa and Napa. We went to morning Mass at one of the big parishes in Napa, and he observed that no one recognized him or cared who he was. He said, "The heart of the Church is never the bishop, but the parish." Pope Francis also gave a homily last week in which he asked, "Is your parish community warm, welcoming and focused on Jesus, or is it just concerned about keeping the commandments?" Hopefully, our parish can answer that rightly and will continue to do so.

This weekend besides Mother's Day, we also have the Annual Appeal for Catholic Charities of the East Bay. I encourage your generous support. Catholic Charities is one of the largest social service providers in the East Bay. It is the social service arm of the Diocese of Oakland and has been serving East Bay families in need since 1935 (that's 78 years!) In 2012, Catholic

Charities served 3,161 clients in Alameda and Contra Costa Counties and also provided important information and referrals to 10,829 individuals in need. In our name, Catholic Charities serves all in need, regardless of their religious affiliation. That includes those about to lose their homes, low-income families in crisis, families and young victims of violence, immigrants and refugees in transition, and those looking for a "hand-up" through work force training. Please be as generous as you can in today's second collection.

Our Parish Council met last weekend to review our annual financial report, which we'll make available to all parishioners next weekend, and to discuss the future development of facilities on our parish plant. For the present, the focus seems to be on our Adult Ministry Center and the need for seismic retrofitting and more room for ministries and volunteers. More on that later.

Happy Mother's Day and God Bless.

Tabernacles-Do
They Get in the Way?

Bulletin Letter — July 18, 1999

My summer experience of Church has included liturgies here at Christ the King with tabernacle off-center and slightly recessed, Mass at Boston College with the tabernacle in a distant and almost undetectable niche, Mass at Chatham, Cape Cod, with the tabernacle at a highly visible side altar, and Mass in our own parish hall (thanks to the new paint job) with no tabernacle or Blessed Sacrament at all. It leads me to some surprising reflections on the place of the tabernacle and the Catholic Church's current regulation that it be in a dignified site, but never in the main Church, unless no other arrangement is possible. Now, isn't that fairly surprising for those of us raised in a generation encouraged to "visit the Blessed Sacrament" before, after and quite possibly during(!) the celebration of the Mass. It really forces us to ask again, "What is the Mass?" and "What is this celebration of Eucharist we are doing?"

Here's the answer in brief outline. It applies to the Last Supper of Jesus, to centuries of the "old Latin Mass," and to the very next Mass you'll be celebrating: (1) We gather together in faith (which usually takes song, processions, greetings exchanged and prayer together). (2) We hear again the story of faith and the Word of the Lord proclaimed (Scripture readings and hopefully the homily too!). (3) We take bread and wine, blessed and shared as sacrifice of praise with the real presence of Christ and one another (Eucharistic prayer and communion). (4) We are sent forth to live out what we've just celebrated; the bread and wine are really changed, not first to be reserved or worshipped, but so that the people who consume this food may become more fully what they already are: the body of Christ.

My own favorite summary of the Eucharist is: "Gather the folks, tell the story, break the bread, change the world!"

Now here's the problem with tabernacles. If we celebrate Eucharist too closely or in the obvious vicinity of a tabernacle, we can concentrate on the presence of Christ independent of whether we show up or not, rather than seeing and celebrating ourselves (as St. Augustine taught) as the ultimate "real presence," sent to change the world. I'll be the first to affirm and reverence the presence of Christ in the tabernacle. I delight in private prayer time before the Blessed Sacrament and the devotions of Benediction and Holy Hour. But, the Catholic Church suggests (and I see the point) that it is difficult to celebrate ourselves transformed by Eucharistic celebration into the Body of Christ *and* to cope with tabernacles at the same time. Historically, the Catholic cathedrals of Europe have dealt with this by placing the tabernacle in dignified chapels far removed from main altar and Eucharistic celebration. You'll never see the Pope celebrate Mass anywhere near a tabernacle. One Chicago parish moved the tabernacle to a place out of sight of the altar and then moved the old communion railing to the back of the church, behind the last pew. This is an effective way to show the congregation that they are the sanctuary, the holy place, as the holy—and responsible—people. The best we can do at Christ the King at the present (encouraged by Church regulations that say it's O.K., if no other arrangement is possible) is to keep readjusting our thinking so that we come to Mass not to observe or even adore Christ in the Eucharist, but to praise God with him and to become with Christ and one another that Eucharistic community, that body of Christ called to transform our neighborhoods and our world.

Marriage and Weddings in the Church

Bulletin Letter — July 12, 1998

Summer is a time for weddings and also a lot of questions about marriage policies and church practice. Here are a few answers. I hope they're helpful.

The recognized or *valid form of marriage* for a baptized Catholic is often called being married "in the Church." That phrase does not refer to the physical location of the wedding (marriages "in the church" have taken place in homes and outdoors). Rather it refers to its acceptance and recognition by the Roman Catholic community. The form a marriage "in the Church" normally takes is for the couple to exchange of in the presence of (1) an authorized representative of the Church (usually a priest or deacon delegated by the local pastor) and (2) two adult witnesses (usually the best man and maid of honor).

The vows may be exchanged briefly in a small chapel with only the couple, the priest, and witnesses present, or in a massive church filled with guests, music, flowers and nuptial Mass. But the essentials are simple and the same. For a Catholic, such an exchange of vows "in the Church" means that the marriage is a sacrament recognized not only by the state, but by the Catholic community as well. When Catholics are not married "in the Church," their marriage is civil and legal, but it is not celebrated as a valid sacrament by our Church, and a question is raised about the appropriateness of subsequently receiving other sacraments, such as communion, until the marriage is blessed "in the Church." It does happen that Catholics not married "in the Church" on occasion do continue to receive communion. This is usually an exception, because of good faith, pursuit of an annulment, or having done all that is possible in good conscience.

Weddings celebrated *outside of the physical church building* (in private houses, gardens, reception halls) are a rarity in the U.S. Priests or deacons can seldom receive authorization to participate. Exceptions to this are Jewish-Christian marriages and rural dioceses where church buildings are few. The thinking behind this common policy is: (1) the symbolism that the event is not a private family affair but belongs to the entire Church community, (2) abuses in the past where home weddings became the sign of wealthy "first class parishioners," and parish church celebrations the sign of poorer, "second-class Catholics," and (3) the experience of restaurants, hotels and reception halls turning the sacramental celebration into a business and marketing event.

Interfaith or *"mixed marriages"* are very common. Of the last twenty weddings celebrated at Christ the King, ten were interfaith. Many years ago, if a Catholic married a non-Catholic "in the Church," both were required to sign a promise that all children would be baptized and raised as Catholics. This is no longer true, although the issue of the children's faith remains an important one. Today, the non-Catholic is not asked to make any promise, but is aware that the Catholic agrees to a cautiously worded phrase "to do all in my power" to see that offspring are raised in the Catholic faith. Exactly what "all in my power" means may vary with different couples, but the issue needs serious discussion prior to any wedding. *Ecumenical wedding celebrations* are common and easy with a little early planning. We are happy to have ministers of other faiths participate by scripture reading, homily or nuptial blessing. In cases where the non-Catholic is extremely close to the Protestant minister or congregation, after all the normal marriage preparation and a specific request to the bishop, non-Catholic clergy may be authorized to represent the Church and the wedding "in the Church" may actually be celebrated in another denomination and by a Protestant minister.

Divorce and *previous marriages* raise the hardest questions, involving frequent misconceptions, and require a great deal of lead time before any subsequent marriage "in the Church." The single most common misunderstanding by Catholics is the misconception that a non-Catholic previously married before a judge or minister ("outside the Church") is free to remarry in a Catholic ceremony, because they were never married "in the Church." Not so! The requirement of a priest and two witnesses for being married "in the Church" is about Catholics and the Catholic community. In practice, this means that any previous marriage of a non-Catholic is seen as *permanent* and *valid*. The rather lengthy process (ten-to-twelve months) of a Church annulment would be necessary before any Catholic ceremony could be planned for a subsequent marriage. We also take the civil marriages ("outside the Church") of Catholics seriously. Although a Church annulment is not necessary prior to a subsequent marriage "in the Church," the simpler process of obtaining a *declaration of freedom to marry* may take up to two months.

This may all seem a bit complicated, especially when most bridal books and wedding guides today do not even mention the possibility of a Church wedding or religious ceremony. But, our community takes marriage very seriously even if that means a lot of extra time and effort. It also suggests that in a sacrament so important for our community and society some other judgments and standards enter in besides what the bride and groom and their immediate family think best. We do not accept that marriage is a private, isolated, "nobody's business but my own" kind of event. The role of parish priest and staff is to help people through all this to careful preparation and a faith-filled celebration.

Annulments and the Church

Bulletin Letter — June 22, 1997

In the last few months, there has been considerable publicity about marriage annulments granted by the Catholic Church, most of it pretty negative. In a recent book and media tour Sheila Rausch Kennedy, who is appealing the church annulment of her twelve year marriage to Rep. Joseph Kennedy, II, lambastes the annulment process as a moral corruption. In a front page article in the *Sunday Examiner* a Catholic layman states that "no power on earth can convince me that I was not married," so he refuses to seek an annulment of his marriage that lasted thirteen years. In an opinion piece in the *Contra Costa Times*, a Protestant woman reports that by getting a church annulment twenty years after their marriage ended, her ex-husband "finally managed to break my heart." She concludes, "Where do they get off declaring that a marriage of two Lutherans in a Lutheran Church never happened?"

Personally, I find these comments quite understandable, but they also miss the meaning and purpose of annulments entirely. Official church language on the subject strongly contributes to the misunderstanding. Industrial-strength phrases like "invalid," "not a true marriage," and "never happened" are thrown around in a kind of church-speak that canon lawyers and theologians may understand correctly, but that actually constitute a misleading misuse of the English language. So, I am going to try to list briefly, in common-sense English, what I believe an annulment is and what it is not. Any canon lawyers listening in are advised to consult an English dictionary and not a canon law book, if they don't understand the following:

(1) An annulment is *not* a claim that your marriage never existed. It did. And, it is a permanent part of your life story. It

was a valid, licensed, legal marriage contract, and your children are forever both legitimate and precious. An annulment does not change that, nor does it claim to change that.

(2) An annulment is a finding *in the name of the Church* that your marriage did not become that "sacrament," "permanent community of love," or "two in one flesh," which Church and Bible hope for and to which newlyweds pledge themselves. In my experience, divorce is usually chosen only for serious reasons and after enormous pain. Most couples would agree well before a divorce is final that there was something substantially amiss with their marriage. "Permanent community of love" would not be an accurate description of their relationship.

(3) An annulment is not a solution to the hurt and unfairness that often accompanies divorce. Nor is it meant to be a justification of irresponsible behavior in a marriage. Some report that the annulment process brings healing, peace, and much-needed closure, but this is not always the case, nor is it the intended purpose of annulments.

(4) An annulment is necessary for both Catholics and non-Catholics who have been previously married, before any subsequent marriage can be celebrated or blessed in the Catholic Church. Our Church recognizes and respects the marriage of two non-Catholics, whether celebrated in their own church or in a civil ceremony.

This recognition and respect raises the same questions about divorce and remarriage that Catholics married in a Catholic ceremony must address:

(1) An annulment is possible only after there is clearly no hope of reconciliation. A civil divorce must be final and obligations of support be met before a petition for annulment is accepted.

(2) An annulment is *not expensive.* In our Diocese, court costs come to $500. If an applicant is unable to pay, court costs are waived. If the final decision is not affirmative, payments that have been made are returned!

Approximately 50,000 annulments are granted in the U.S. each year. Oakland granted 390 in the last two years, while the San Francisco Archdiocese granted 420 during the same period. The average time from first interview to decision is six-to-eight months.

The whole annulment process raises problems, but they are not the ones reported in the *Sunday Examiner* and *Contra Costa Times* articles. To my mind, those comments arise from a misunderstanding and mistaken notion of annulments. While 75 percent of all Church annulments are granted in the U.S., I do not feel that the large number of U.S. annulments of themselves constitute a problem. The Church in our country is willing to spend $20 million a year on court expenses to apply the policies and procedures which the Vatican and Church law give as a right to every Catholic.

One problem raised by annulments stems from the claim of Church management and tribunals that the marriage *"never existed."* This use of Church-speak instead of common-sense English angers good Catholics and puzzles non-Catholics. It is closer to the truth to say that the Church, in the name of a believing community and as a concerned spokesperson for the value of permanence in marriage (as opposed to a civil court), recognizes that there was something substantially amiss, that there was no hope of reconciliation, and that people need to be freed to move on with their lives.

The second and major problem raised by annulments is how to keep a delicate balance between support, forgiveness, and hope for couples whose marriages have ended, and even stronger support for couples who are struggling to be faithful to their marriage and marriage vows. Pre-marital counseling, six-month engagement requirements, marriage preparation weekends, courses for couples approaching marriage, and programs such as Marriage Encounter and Retrovaille for couples already married are some of the ways the Church tries to keep that balance.

Evolution, Science, and the Church

Bulletin Letter — July 25, 1999

Evolution, Science and the Church seem, much of the time and to many people, very uncomfortable with each other. Despite what you may read in the press or hear trumpeted by fundamentalist Christians, I believe the exact opposite is true.

Evolution is broader and more balanced than the belief that we're all descended from monkeys! It is the highly respected theory that all forms of life descend, with modification, from earlier forms. Some drastic revisions of Darwin's original theory are proposed today, but most scientists accept a similar synthesis of genetics, molecular biology, and Darwin's principles. In an extended sense, "evolution" also refers to the unfolding story of the entire universe.

Despite some initial misgivings, Catholic teaching and theology have been pretty hospitable to the theory of evolution. From the debates at Oxford in 1860 to the Scopes trial in Tennessee in 1925, to the present day campaign for creationism in the classroom, strong hostility to evolution has been largely a Protestant rather than a Catholic concern.

Originally in 1616, the Vatican put the works of Copernicus and Galileo on its Index of Forbidden Books along with "all books teaching that the earth moves and the sun stands still." By the early 1800s, the Pope was personally approving texts that taught precisely that, and the Vatican was quietly and bashfully removing those titles from its forbidden list—well before the appearance of Darwin and his theories. With the arrival of Darwin, despite some concern and caution, there were no ringing condemnations from Rome and no rush to forbid the reading of evolutionary literature. In 1909, the Vatican's Commission on Scripture agreed that no one was bound to the literal words of Genesis with its seven-day version of creation. The Church was echoing the view of leaders 300 years earlier who said, "The Bible teaches us how to go to heaven, not how the heavens go." In 1950, Pope Pius XII cautiously and officially recognized evolution as a plausible theory. In 1994, under Pope John Paul II, the *New Catholic Catechism* complimented science for "splendidly enriching our knowledge of the age and dimensions of the universe, the development of life forms and the appearance of human beings."

Today, Catholic theology is quite comfortable with the view that God "creates" *through* evolution. It distances itself from "creationism," which insists on a literalist view of the seven days of creation or the instant version. It also disagrees with "creation science" or "scientific creationism," which considers the Bible a more reliable source for scientific information than modern evolutionary biology. The Catholic community leaves lots of room for a variety of personal beliefs about the world's start-up. Its teaching also allow generous room for the possibility of evolution as the means of God's creative action.

Because of their concentration on social justice and human freedom, Catholic teachers and theologians have not spent a great deal of time or print on just how evolution fits in. But it's safe to say that contemporary Catholic theologians maintain a high respect for scientific study and theory. They see the data of evolutionary science as consistent with the Bible's God of compassionate love and persuading power. They consider the random nature of evolution as compatible with a God who loves freedom and lets the world be. They recognize in the loss and suffering of our evolving universe the self-emptying God revealed in the cross of Christ.

For myself, I take both the Bible (study of God) and science (study of nature) seriously, recalling as St. Thomas Aquinas taught, "Making a mistake about nature leads to making a mistake about God."

The Death of the Death Penalty?

Bulletin Letter — July 16, 2000

According to one commentator, "Historians of the 21st century may well identify 1999 as a watershed year in the long drive to abolish the death penalty in the U.S." Another columnist wrote last month, "The death of the death penalty may occur in Rome on July 9th. On that Sunday the pope will visit a prison and call for a moratorium on the death penalty." The momentum and clarity of Catholic Church teaching in opposition to the death penalty has certainly accelerated in the last two years. John Paul II made his first public plea to the U.S. to end execution. The U.S. Catholic bishops issued a collective statement in opposition to the death penalty. The pope revised section 2266 of the *Catholic Catechism* to remove the statement that capital punishment could be allowed "in cases of extreme necessity" and instead to describe it as "cruel and unnecessary," to be admitted only if it is the sole alternative.

In Pennsylvania, the Cardinal and all bishops called for a moratorium. In Washington, the state's bishops did the same with the concession, "Some Catholics may not be aware of how the Church's teaching about capital punishment has developed." The bishops of North Carolina issued a similar statement on Good Friday. The Catholic bishops of Texas have confronted Governor Bush, asking him to suspend executions with 463 prisoners awaiting it in his state. Cardinal Keeler of Washington, D.C., issued a joint Jewish/Catholic statement in opposition. The president of the Philippines declared a moratorium in response to the country's bishops. And these are only a few examples.

However, while the Church's official teaching has crystallized against the death penalty, a majority of American

Catholics (only 30% of whom think the death penalty is morally wrong) and Americans at large continue to support the practice. Their reasons include the need to make restitution, fear of the offender being released from prison, and a belief that death deters others as well as the person convicted of the crime. The emotional, relational, and even faith testing aspects of what victims of murder and their loved ones experience must be acknowledged. Murder is a grave, irreversible offense against life.

Here are some points to consider and possible action to take in the light of the revised Catechism statement, "The cases in which the execution of the offender is an absolute necessity are very rare, if not practically non-existent."

(1) The argument for deterrence has never been established. Attorney General Janet Reno, a life-long prosecutor, said on January 20th, "I have inquired for most of my adult life about studies that might show that the death penalty is a deterrent. And I have not seen any research that would substantiate that point."

(2) Execution of the innocent has been established. Since 1976 at least 85 people on death row have been belatedly proved innocent and released.

(3) Life imprisonment without possibility of parole has proven to work and can be implemented, if the legislative will and popular support are present (plus, for concerned taxpayers it has proven a less expensive way to go).

(4) Church teaching has developed over the centuries in relation to changing social conditions and currently focuses on the "consistent ethic of life" that insists every life is sacred, not just the lives of the good.

A Moratorium 2000 movement has been organized with the hope that one million signatures on a petition will be delivered by Sr. Helen Prejean to the United Nations on Human Rights Day, December 10th. We'll let you know more about ways to sign the petition in the early fall.

A "Dysfunctional" Church?

Bulletin Letter — July 9, 1995

Frequently these days, the term "dysfunctional" is used of individuals, families and institutions. Sometimes effective and sometimes not, it is an effort to name built-in patterns of behavior that are ultimately destructive. The term has even been used of the institutional Church. That's a little unsettling at first, because we believe that the side of Church which is Spirit-driven and gospel-faithful can never be anything but healthy and life-giving. But, it is part of our traditional Catholic faith to believe that the Church in its humanness can be quite mistaken, misguided, corrupt and, yes, even "dysfunctional." One of the more famous symptoms is denial, the refusal to admit or discuss real problems. AA and Alanon groups refer to "the elephant in the middle of the room," a problem everyone knows is there but no one ever mentions. Over the last year at least three issues (are they "elephants in the middle of the room"?) have been addressed in the Church not just by journalists, critics, and gum chewing Catholics, but by the hierarchy, prominent bishops and leaders of our Church at its management level.

(1) **Divorced, Remarried Catholics and Communion** - In the fall of 1993, three prominent, conservative and highly respected German bishops issued a joint statement that divorced and remarried Catholics should receive pastoral help and not be banned from the sacraments. That is a position, I suspect, which has the silent approval of the majority of other bishops and almost all moral theologians. The three bishops made several visits to the Vatican to discuss their views. Last fall, the Vatican issued its response that any previous marriage should first be annulled. The president of the German bishops' conference has responded that this is "a harsh answer," and it is clear that the

bishops do not see the discussion as over or the possibility of more open pastoral approaches ruled out.

(2) **Celibacy and the Priesthood** - Irish bishops are speaking out! Bishop Comiskey of Ferns recently declared that we must "start seriously considering" a change to allow married priests. Bishop Walsh of Killaloe commented that he saw no conflict between a man being a priest and husband and father, as well. Meanwhile, Cardinal Martini of Milan called celibacy a historical decision that could be reconsidered, and the retired Cardinal of Vienna recommended a change.

(3) **Silence in the Official Church** - Last month 40 U.S. bishops endorsed a twelve-page statement calling for a more open discussion between bishops' conferences and Rome on controversial issues. It questioned whether "collegiality" was a reality or an illusion. The examples it gave included changes by Vatican officials of U.S. statements on women, on the translation to English of the *Catholic Catechism*, and on women's ordination. All without any prior discussion or consultation with the U.S. Bishops' Conference.

Discussion rather than denial seems to me to be both healthy and holy. Even though the examples are limited to the past rather than the present, Pope John Paul has given considerable leadership here. In an address to the College of Cardinals last year, he called for public acknowledgement of past errors. He has confessed error in the Galileo case, drawn a straight line between methods of the Inquisition and those of Stalin and Hitler, called the Church to correct the record on John Huss, a Church reformer burned at the stake in 1415. He has deplored the Church's involvement in the slave trade, asked pardon for the Church's failure to bring just treatment to the native peoples of the Americas, condemned the excesses of the Crusades, and visited a Roman synagogue to apologize for the wrongs of the Inquisition.

Being "dysfunctional" sure gives you a lot to talk about!

Fired Up About Cremation

Bulletin Note — 2001

For centuries, Roman Catholics did not accept cremation as a way of burial except in emergency situations such as plague or public necessity. The roots of this opposition go back to three sources: 1) a strong belief in the body as precious and the temple of the Holy Spirit; 2) the view from early Christian days that cremation was a pagan practice in opposition to Christian beliefs; and, 3) the choice of cremation both early on and in much more recent centuries as a symbolic way of denying the resurrection of the dead. However, in our lifetime, since 1963 (that's for the last 38 years!), the Church has officially allowed cremation along with Christian burial and its popularity (if that's the right word) among Catholics has grown steadily. An estimated 20 percent of all funerals in the United States involve cremation. However, here at Christ the King, and probably in all our neighboring parishes, the percentage is much higher— at least 50 percent and possibly more. We've had five funerals scheduled this week, from Monday to Monday, and all five included cremation.

Obviously times have changed and the ancient reasons for opposition to cremation seldom if ever apply any more. Families choose cremation for economic reasons, for convenience for distant relatives to have time to arrive, for practical, pastoral reasons that have nothing whatsoever to do with pagan practices, denial of resurrection, or disrespect for the body. The Church's decision to allow cremation recognizes that sometimes it best meets the needs of the family.

The celebration of funeral rites around cremation take a variety of forms, but for that matter, funerals with the body present also take a variety of forms today. In some cases there is a funeral vigil, and funeral Mass with the body present, followed by cremation and a placing of the ashes in the Catholic cemetery at a later date. More often cremation takes place early on. A memorial Mass is scheduled at the convenience of the family, sometimes with cremains present, sometimes without. A picture of the deceased is often placed near the altar. The remains are most often placed at the Catholic cemetery with a brief graveside ceremony. In other cases, the family retains the ashes.

The rituals of our Church adapt (sometimes a bit slowly) to the cultural needs of its members. Sometimes, the outward rites change, but basic beliefs and values are not sacrificed. Above all, as parish and Church we need to support one another through grief and honor the life and memory of the departed.

Politics and Our Beloved Dead

Bulletin Letter — November 3, 2002

The month of November is traditionally marked by two concerns. Both, believe it or not, are spiritual and religious realities. One is the remembrance of our beloved dead, the other is politics with November elections.

Let me begin with the more religious of the two, elections and politics!! After all, Jesus spent a lot of his teaching on what we do for the least of our neighbors, how we love one another, and how we put his wisdom and values into practice. Healthy religion is very much about compassion, service, and justice which are concrete and practical. Political decisions are a big part of how we put that into practice. Or as Pope Paul VI said, "Politics is the highest form of charity"! While there are plenty of issues and propositions that do not have a major moral dimension, many do. Let me repeat here, just short of an election day, the five steps I suggest (by now they should be familiar) that Catholic Christians need to take when facing value-laden, publically moral (that usually means political) decisions.

1) Stay in touch with and keep going back to Jesus, his words, his stories, his teaching, his wisdom.

2) Do our homework and get the facts as best we can (morality after all is based on reality, on getting it right).

3) Insist on and welcome our spiritual leaders, specifically our bishops, speaking out on major issues with moral dimensions or touching on basic human rights.

4) Reflect not just on their conclusions, but on their reasons and arguments.

5) Then, follow our own best judgment, our conscience. If that judgment is in disagreement with our spiritual leaders, so

be it; but keep the door wide open for revisiting our decision, if there is new information.

November is also a time to remember our loved ones who have died. All Souls Day envelopes, available in the vestibule, and the "Book of Our Beloved Dead" in the front of church are two reminders. A Bereavement Mass for those who have died in the recent past will be celebrated next Sunday. And a remembrance ceremony for Msgr. Wade (d. November 1, 1999) and Margo Schorno (d. November 16, 1999) will be held at Queen of Heaven Cemetery on Tuesday, November 12. But, exactly where and how are our departed loved ones? I repeat from my Easter letter in 2000:

What about the 'resurrection' and future of our deceased loved ones? The words and message of a Jesus who is risen and his followers who have experienced his continuing presence is a pretty good assurance, 'a blessed assurance,' that our loved ones live one. I find it also confirming and reassuring that modern science describes a universe:

(1) where nothing is ever lost. The old view of a three-story world with an upstairs space for 'heaven' is long gone, replaced by 'billions and billions of galaxies'; but it is a universe where even the smallest atoms and energy are never lost and where Stephen Hawking (A Brief History of Time) can describe life continuing in another dimension.

(2) where there is a new-found sense of the universe as a journey, rather than a random series of stops and starts, and a universe that accumulates and progresses rather than turns backwards and loses what it has achieved (like human lives!);

(3) where at the heart of each person's life is consciousness and relationship that I believe is never lost. Our loved ones live on.

Thoughts on the Devil and Hell

Bulletin Letter — July 27, 2003

It must be the heat! I want to share a few summertime thoughts on the devil and hell! Two related and slightly surprising items made the news in recent years. One was the result of two major polls that showed belief in the devil is more widespread in the U.S. than it's ever been since pollsters began asking the question in the 1950s. The second item was the description by news reporters and evangelical leaders of Pope John Paul II as "soft-selling hell" and making it just "a state of mind."

During the high temperatures of the last two weeks, my own hell-bent thoughts went to the cartoon showing two men standing up to their waists in hell fire with one of them commenting, "But it's a dry heat!"

The biblical authors were neither stenographers for God nor eyewitness reporters on the physical conditions of the Afterlife. Instead, they were inspired and passionate about communicating their faith convictions in language and a world view familiar to their intended audience. Two things about the biblical descriptions of hell:

1) while important and endlessly provocative, it always points toward a reality that remains beyond our comprehension;

2) it keeps changing: there's "Gehenna," first a valley southwest of Jerusalem where children had been sacrificed to a pagan God, later a burning garbage area; there's a place "of weeping and gnashing of teeth"; there's St. Paul's negative description that the truly wicked have no place in the kingdom. Pope John Paul II says, "Sacred Scripture uses many images to describe the pain, frustration, and emptiness of life without God."

Most people today find it hard to think of heaven as a place of happiness up in the sky or of hell as a fiery furnace down below. As one major theologian, Karl Rahner, puts it: the biblical images of hell are not graphic previews or detailed pictures of the fate of the wicked. Rather, they are metaphors meant to reveal deeper truths about our existence as free creatures responsible to a Divine Judge. Our essential freedom allows us to say a final and definitive "no" to the loving God who relentlessly pursues us. And separation from that God would be the ultimate tragedy.

According to Pope John Paul II, "Hell is not a punishment imposed externally by God, but the condition resulting from attitudes and activities people adopt in their life"; hell is more than a physical place and is better understood as the state of those who freely and definitely separate themselves from God, the source of all life and joy."

It is also worth remembering that the Bible insists that wherever sin exists, forgiveness and grace even more abound. Heaven and hell are not equal options. The flow of the universe is toward fulfillment and unity with its Creator, not ultimate alienation and estrangement. Saying no to God is contrary to our authentic impulses and our best instincts. We need only remember our basic *Baltimore Catechism* question: "Why did God make me?" The divine plan is to restore all things in Christ.

One modern theologian, known for his generally conservative view and his strong influence with the Vatican, was Hans Urs von Balthasar. Before his death in 1988, he published a surprising book entitled, "Dare We Hope?" He argues that we can at least hope that all human beings are ultimately saved because of the immensity and power of divine love.

If this summer heat continues, I'll write about the devil next week!

The Devil (Continued)

Bulletin Letter — August 3, 2003

"The devil, you say!" The summer heat continues, and as promised, as I'll share a few thoughts on the devil.

Contrary to media wisdom, a belief in the devil is widespread, even among the nation's best educated. Two polls released in March (Gallup and Harris) agree that belief in "the devil" is as high in the U.S. as it's ever been since they began asking the question in the 1950s. Both polls reported the same 68 percent number, well over the 51 percent reported a dozen years ago. Neither of the polls define what people mean by the "devil." In a 1978 poll, Gallup found that half the respondents were talking about "a personal being, who directs evil forces and influences people to do wrong." The other half describes the devil as "an impersonal force that influences people to do wrong."

Surprisingly, the Bible gives us considerably less help than we might expect when it comes to "devil talk." The devil is not an important figure in the Old Testament. The word appears in only five books (out of 46) and is mentioned only once in four of them. The famous snake in the Garden of Eden was not meant to symbolize the devil, and in the story of Job the character called Satan acts as a court appointed attorney to present human failings to a heavenly tribunal. Satan is not equal to God and not described as an evil power.

The devil is much more active in the New Testament. The Gospel writers use terms like "Evil One," "Father of Lies," "Murderer from the Beginning." The devil seems to have limited power to cause sickness and the temptation to sin. However, it cannot cause moral wrongs or corruption, does not know Christ's true identity, and must obey the word of

Christ and his disciples. The New Testament indicates that it is difficult to separate the evil that results from devils and that which results from human choice, but in any case the coming of Christ overwhelms the power of the devil.

Reference to the devil appears very seldom in official Catholic statements of faith, and the devil is not mentioned in any official Christian creed.

Personally, I think belief in "the devil" is often either understated or overstated.

Understated – If we still carry around that cartoon figure of a pitchfork-wielding and red-tailed devil whispering in people's ears, I think we underestimate by far the cosmic power that undermines our best instincts and multiplies the evil we do with demonic force. Evil is real. Its consequences can be enormous, and it often increases almost geometrically.

Overstated – To think that the power of evil is an equal factor with the power of God is to misunderstand both the gospel and the universe of God's creation. To attribute our evil choices to an outside agent ("the devil made me do it") is to duck our own very real responsibility for good and bad in the world.

One of my favorite quotes is attributed to C.S. Lewis who wrote that marvelous little book, *The Screwtape Letters*, in which the older devil, Uncle Screwtape, advises his nephew devil Wormword on how best to tempt people and lead people astray. When complimented on his insights about the work of the devil, Lewis is said to have responded, "Oh that book is not about the devil, no, it's about the human heart!"

Msgr. Philip J. Murnion

Bulletin Letter — August 21, 2003

Last weekend I made a quick two-day trip to New York City to attend the Vigil Service and Funeral Mass for Msgr. Philip J. Murnion. For the past thirty years, Phil has been a little- known but enormously significant leader in the U.S. Catholic Church. For me, since 1969, he has been a very close and dear friend.

A priest of the Archdiocese of New York, he was founder and director of the National Pastoral Life Center. The Center was established in 1983 to serve parishes and pastoral leadership of the Church from pastors to pastoral ministers, diocesan personnel, and bishops. As part of his personal gifts and part of the Center's work, he helped bring R.C.I.A. to fruition in our country, served as editor of *Church Magazine*, developed national courses for new pastors, established a highly regarded annual convention for pastoral leaders, served as inspiration and consultant to the Roundtable Associates of Social Action Directors across the U.S., and directed the Common Ground Initiative, which the late Cardinal Bernardin of Chicago began in 1996 to foster dialogue in the Church.

As a priest- sociologist, he conducted groundbreaking studies of parish developments, pastoral ministries, and the Notre Dame study of Parish Life, as well as directing the U.S. Bishops' five-year Parish Project.

While not well known or highly publicized among average Catholic parishioners, Phil, his Center, and his vision have had great influence on parish life and pastoral leaders. He was quite possibly the only Church leader in the U.S. with such extensive and effective connection with practically every major national Church association for ministry, as well as acceptance and support from a high number of U.S. bishops and their National

Conference. Phil was a dedicated and determined "centrist" in a Church torn by extremes and polarized by debate from left and right. The work of the Center he founded will continue the vision and pastoral service to which he devoted his life.

I came to know Phil well when we lived together for two years (1969-70) at St. Gregory's in New York. He was earning his doctorate in sociology at Columbia, as I pursued graduate studies in theology and education at Manhattan College. Since those dear and exciting days, we never lost contact.

Last October I spent three days as a presenter along with him at his annual Pastoral Leadership Convention in Louisville, Kentucky. During my recent ten-week sabbatical, I stayed a for a week with him at the Holy Name Center for Homeless Men in New York's Bowery, the place where he housed the Center and called home for the past two decades. Just three weeks ago, I made a lightning visit to New York for a quickly called one-day meeting of the Center's Board of Trustees and a one-hour visit with Phil at the NYU Medical Center and Hospital. Typically for Phil, much of the conversation and all of his concern was about me and my welfare, rather than about him and his health. I still have on my answering machine his last call to me, when he phoned to ask how I was doing and quietly added, "I'm not doing so well myself."

At the Vigil Service, his brother recounted how Phil awoke late at night in his hospice bed surrounded by family members. When told what the time was he said, "Go home; go home; you should all be at home." Then he added, "I want you to stay, but go home!" His brother then concluded by addressing Phil's remains, "We want you to stay, but go home, Phil, go home!"

Phil was 65, celebrated his 40th anniversary as a priest this year, and passed away after a year-and-a-half struggle with colon cancer. It was a struggle that barely slowed him down until his very last days.

His death is a great loss for the Church, for parish life, and certainly for me personally. I just wanted you to know.

Msgr. Philip J. Murnion's Letter to U.S. Bishops

Bulletin Letter — September 7, 2003

Two days before his death, Msgr. Philip J. Murnion sent a letter to all the bishops of the United States. Following are excerpts:

"In his final public address on Oct. 24, 1996, Cardinal Joseph Bernardin spoke these moving words: 'A dying person does not have time for the peripheral or the accidental. He or she is drawn to the essential, the important—yes, the eternal. And what is important, my friends, is that we find that unity with the Lord and within the community of faith for which Jesus prayed so fervently on the night before he died . . . .'"

"Now in God's providence, I too write this reflection as a dying person with no time for the peripheral or accidental. In many ways, the crisis in the church and the ensuing polarization, which so preoccupied Cardinal Bernardin, have only grown more acute. Your own credibility and ability to guide God's people have been severely compromised . . . ."

"In the mind of the Pope, there is no contradiction between legitimate authority and careful consultation . . . . Consultation, listening, and dialogue only enhance true authority, because they issue from a lived trust and they serve to increase trust. It is imperative that we work together to restore the trust that has been eroded."

"If I were to sum up my final plea to you, it would be: 'dialogue, dialogue, dialogue!' I do not mean this as a facile or pious slogan, for I am only too aware of its cost and conditions."

"A spirituality of communion and dialogue is as demanding in its asceticism as a spirituality of the desert or the cloister. Like them, it also requires its own appropriate structures. The Catholic tradition knows well that spirituality and structure are not opposed. Here, as elsewhere, it affirms the 'both/and' of charism and institution, invisible grace and visible embodiment. Both are essential, though only one is eternal. We can ill afford to be less Catholic than the Pope himself, who insists: 'The spirituality of communion, by prompting a trust and openness wholly in accord with the dignity and responsibility of every member of the people of God, supplies institutional reality with a soul.'"

"For more than 20 years, I have been blessed by working with many of you in different programs of the National Pastoral Life Center. I know from experience that many have sought diligently to consult and communicate with your priests and people alike. But, in this time of crisis, of both possibility and peril, we face the urgent need imaginatively to expand present structures and to create new ones that will enable us to draw more effectively upon the rich wisdom of those baptized . . . .'"

"Permit me, then, with the last breaths the Spirit gives me to implore you: Do not be afraid to embrace this spirituality of communion, this 'little way' of dialogue with one another, with your priests, with all God's faithful. Doing so, you will touch not only the hearts of your brothers and sisters; you will draw closer to the very heart of Jesus, the Lord and brother of us all . . . ."

Fr. Bill O'Donnell
January 2, 1930 – December 8, 2003

Bulletin Letter — December 28, 2003

On December 8th of this year, I lost a long-time and dear friend. Our Church and community lost a larger-than-life character and controversial hero. Newspaper reports described him as "the saint of the labor movement" and "the conscience of Berkeley." Bill would have quickly laughed off any such praise, but he spent most of his life challenging us and standing up for causes, when most people looked the other way. His close friend Martin Sheen of *West Wing* fame once said of him, "Bill is one of the scariest people I know, because he makes us tell the truth, the whole truth, and nothing but the truth, all the time. He takes the cup as it is offered, not altered." His 225 arrests for civil disobedience around issues of human rights, peace, nuclear disarmament, union causes, farm workers' rights and the School of the Americas are strong evidence of that. He saw the sacred in the downtrodden and never tired of fighting for their rights.

For all of his commitment to non-violence, deep down I think Bill always loved a good fight. He had both a talent and a zest for disturbing us. At priests' convocations and study days, the one thing you could always count on was a challenge from the floor from Bill O'Donnell, "holy heckler" that he loved to be.

One of my fondest memories of Bill is spending much of a day last January, along with Fr. Brian Timoney and Gwen Watson, in the visiting room with him at Atwater Federal Penitentiary. At age 73, Bill spent six months in that high security federal prison in Merced for trespassing in protest of The School of the Americas in Fort Benning, Georgia. The School stands accused of training secret police and military of Latin America in both tactics and torture. Bill had, after a few weeks in prison, already formed Bible study sessions and discussion groups on non-violence. He also told me that he was hearing more confessions in prison than he ever had at the parish.

I was at his welcome-home celebration in March, where a standing room only Church sang, "O where have you been Billy Boy, Billy Boy, O where have you been charming Billy?" At his first Mass after his release (he was forbidden to celebrate Mass in prison or, as the warden said, "Don't do any of that religious stuff"), he urged parishioners not to shrug at injustice and say, "What's the use?" "The opposite of faith," he said, "is not doubt, but fatalism."

A week after his release, he was arrested (but not jailed) for protesting the war in Iraq. Just a few weeks ago, he was at Fort Benning, along with 10,000 others, to once again protest the School of the Americas.

Along the way Bill also found time to serve as pastor of St. Joseph the Worker from 1973 to 1995, to co-found the San Carlos Foundation, which brings aid to villages of Central America, and to work closely and first hand at "Options Recovering Services"—with hardcore alcoholics and drug addicts who are often homeless and suffering from mental illness. At his own request, Bill was buried in a plain wooden coffin in a pauper's grave.

For me Bill was always inspiration, challenge, and supportive friend. We also laughed a lot together. He is greatly missed.

Response to "Contra Costa Times" Series on Clergy Abuse

Letter Read at Mass April 6, 2008

I'm sure most of you are painfully aware of the four-part series that appeared this week in the *Contra Costa Times* and five other Bay Area newspapers about the Diocese of Oakland and sexual abuse by clergy and religious. The reaction I've heard all week is shock and disappointment, but for a variety of very different reasons.

There is shock and disappointment because the first question is "Why Now? Why on earth now?" While very sad and tragic, most of the information (or news!) is already well known, thoroughly reported, and a matter of public and legal record. Important safeguards, procedures and protocols are now long in place and being carefully followed. There is shock and disappointment, because it stands as a painful reminder that we must say "never again" and recognize there still are some survivors suffering and who are quite unable to be named or to step forward.

There is shock and disappointment at the large number of abusers and that some of them were personally known and well-respected. In many cases appropriate action was taken too little and too late.

There is shock and disappointment, because some whose innocence has been established or who died with no chance to defend themselves are still included, because they were once accused or their name once appeared in a legal brief.

There is shock and disappointment, because listed under the Bishop and Diocese of Oakland is a large number (at least forty) who were never under the authority, responsibility or supervision of the Diocese at any time.

There is shock and disappointment, because it is not made clear that in most (but sadly not all) cases, that those accused were referred to competent professionals, whose advice was closely followed, and the professionals turned out to be wrong.

Finally, it is keenly disappointing that there is no mention that, despite tragic enough mistakes and failures, the Diocese of Oakland was among the first in the nation, well over ten years ago, to conduct public apology services, to publicly encourage victims to step forward, and to organize support groups for survivors of clergy abuse.

Still, the series represents an opportunity for us to acknowledge the pain still prevalent, not only with the survivors but with the church community as a whole. The series gives us an opportunity to revisit our commitment to our children and to be vigilant in our decision for "no more secrets" and to say, "never again". . . an opportunity to admit that we should have been more observant and we could have done more . . . and an opportunity to recognize those survivors who stepped forward as real heroes and that we must be grateful for their courage.

We have a lot of healing to do, a lot to guard against, but overall, I did not find the *Times* series timely, balanced or helpful at all.

Reunion and Lack of Vocations

Bulletin Letter — September 15, 2013

On Thursday of this past week, I hosted a Mass and Reunion Luncheon for those who have been my classmates at St. Joseph's College in Mountain View and St. Patrick's Seminary in Menlo Park, anywhere and anytime between 1951 and 1963. The occasion, I guess, is the 50th ordination anniversary of those who did eventually get ordained. But most of all, it was a chance for all of us to get together to remember and to celebrate.

My Seminary Class at St. Joseph's College, Mt. View, CA, 1954.

When we started as a class in September of 1951, there were almost one hundred of us. Many more both joined and left us over the next twelve years. Finally, in 1963, twenty-two of us were ordained to the priesthood for the dioceses of San Francisco, Oakland, Santa Rosa, Sacramento, Reno and Hawaii.

Of the original members who started in 1951, there were sixteen of the twenty-two who were ordained, which for those days was a high percentage. Usually, one out of ten continued to ordination. In our case, it was one out of six. My recollection is, after the first quarter of that 9th Grade in 1951, we were already reduced to just eighty. In those days the faculty was busy doing everything it possibly could to throw us out. What a difference from today, when vocations are so limited that faculties do everything possible to keep you in!

With the present shortage of vocations to priesthood and disappearing number of women religious (sisters), many feel this is a great loss. Frankly, I feel just the opposite. The great gift and blessing of our time is the recognition and growth of ministries by all our baptized parishioners. Instead of people thinking you have to be a nun or a priest to do ministry, we now recognize that all of us are called to be active, engaged ministers of the Church. The fact that for at least a thousand years there were no teaching nuns and relatively few ordained priests reminds us that for the Church to be alive and well it does not need "religious vocations," but rather the vocations of us all to be ministers who hear the gospel and make a difference. It was impressive to hear from so many classmates the when, where, and how they continue to be active parishioners and collaborate in leadership and ministry in the Church.

Left Behind - The Rapture!

Bulletin Letter — August 19, 2001

A number of parishioners have asked recently about the best-selling *Left Behind* series of novels that makes an industry of the Apocalypse and highlights belief in "the Rapture"—a view of the Bible and mysterious predictions pretty much unknown to the average Catholic. The beliefs about the end of the world that you'll find in these novels is foreign to both the Catholic and traditional Christian approach to either the Bible or the future. Actually, it's almost impossible to find a good Bible scholar to even comment on this fanciful approach, but books, movies and some evangelical Protestants keep these theories in the news, so it's good to know a little more about them.

A Protestant friend advised me that growing up in her church could be scary with nightmares about "the Rapture." In her evangelical church, sermons on "the Rapture" regularly predict that someday, without warning, Christ will snatch away to heaven all the true Christians, leaving behind the unfortunates who would suffer seven years of "tribulation" under the Antichrist. One night, at age eight, she woke up to find her parents gone. She was convinced and terrified that they had been "raptured" and she had been left behind. What a relief to later find out they had just gone out for pizza!

Left Behind novels now number eight and counting. They regularly make the best-seller list and have produced a children's book series, Christian music CDs, radio dramas and *Left Behind: The Movie*. Using chiefly the Book of Daniel, I Thessalonians 4:16-17, and Revelation 20:1-15, they are based on a relatively recent interpretation of the Bible that predicts a detailed description for the end of the world divided into several key eras or "dispensations": the Rapture, the Seven-

Year Tribulation, Christ's return, and the defeat of the Antichrist with his one-world religion, the familiar "mark of the beast," plagues, disaster, millions of Jews converting to Christianity, and the beginning of Christ's 1,000 year reign (the millennium)! All of this thinking has a jawbreaker of a title: "dispensational premillennialism"!! This system of biblical interpretation was developed around 1830 in England by John Nelson Darby. It gained a foothold in the U.S. through Bible study notes written by Cyrus Scofield in 1909 and was popularized in the 1970s by Hal Lindsey's bestseller, *The Late Great Planet Earth*. After about 2,000 years of Christianity, it is a very recent and highly questionable way of reading the Bible.

If you read any of the *Left Behind* series (which I do not recommend), you'll find besides a very unreliable reading of the Bible, (1) a mean-spirited vision of faith (it's your own fault if you don't make the Rapture), (2) a clubbiness with other believers (we're the ones with the truth, you're not), (3) a subtle anti-Catholicism (which is strong and explicit in the author's other writings), (4) a profound distrust of ecumenism (any one-world religion is the work of the Antichrist), (5) a complete disinterest in social justice (any preaching of peace before Jesus returns is the work of the Antichrist!).

While Catholic and mainline Christian teaching speaks of "the last things," with heaven, hell and Last Judgment, it does not claim to have a blueprint or timetable of the final events. The fiery and dramatic symbols of the Book of Revelation have their place in our art, stained glass windows and hymns. But they are taken as metaphors for the victory of Christ over evil, rather than as a secret code to be cracked open after 1,900plus years. Rather than being fanciful, Catholic Biblical scholarship tries to be faithful to what the Scriptures meant to the people who wrote them and to what it might mean to us now. The *Left Behind* novels, which include *Tribulation Force*, *The Indwelling*, and *The Mark: The Beast Rules the World* deserve to be left behind!

The Catholic Top Ten

Homily of January 2, 2000

The feast of the wise men and the beginning of a new year and a new century is a good time to remember and celebrate key figures in our life and in the life of the Church. So, I've prepared my list of the 10 most significant Catholics of the century, at least for the Church and for Catholics in the U.S.

Two that will not make the list either for the century or for the nation, but will certainly be at the top of the list for our parishioners' generation here at CTK, are Msgr. James J. Wade and Margo Schorno.

On my list of 10 for the century, probably the most obvious choice (and the only living person on my list!) is **Pope John Paul II**. His leadership as Pope has spanned 21 years, easily the longest term of office of any pope of the century. He has signaled a new look in papal history with his worldwide travel. His stand for social justice, solidarity, human rights and the defense of life has impacted the politics of our world and has been widely credited for the downfall of Soviet communism. His impact on Church life receives mixed reviews, but it has clearly been enormous, as he has stamped the administration of the Church and its position on in-house issues with his views and a conservatism that will last well into the next century.

Number 2 on my list is **John F. Kennedy**, not because of his politics or personal life, but because of the change he marked and to some extent personally made in the status of Catholics as American citizens. He ran for the presidency in the face of concerted opposition because of his religion and against the accepted political wisdom "that no Catholic could ever be elected president in this country." His election shattered the last political barrier to America's acceptance of Catholics. Catholics no longer had to keep proving they were good citizens by indiscriminate support of everything American. Now, like other citizens, they could be both loyal and critical, supportive and careful. Kennedy's call for us to "ask what we could do for our country" inspired not only the Peace Corps and the War on Poverty, but also similar efforts in the Catholic community for lay volunteers and funding for human development.

My next three choices are less familiar names and faces, but they have shaped the thoughts and conversation of U.S. Catholics with science, with politics, and with spirituality. Without them, our thinking and actions would be considerably different than they are.

Number 3 on my list is **Pierre Teilhard de Chardin**. Teilhard was a French priest, scientist and theologian. He spent much of his life on expeditions to examine prehistoric fossils in China and Africa. When he outlined a theology that brought together faith and science, evolution and spirituality, he was silenced by his Jesuit superiors and by the Vatican. At his death in 1955, only six people attended his funeral. A lone priest went to the cemetery for the burial, and Teilhard's name was misspelled on his tombstone. Then a friend began to publish his writings which have now reached millions. His basic theories have been widely accepted and further developed. The Vatican, by 1960, named him as one of the great thinkers of the century and his thoughts and phrases on the world, evolution, science and humanism found their way into the official teaching of the Second Vatican Council!

Number 4 on my list, **John Courtney Murray**, an American Jesuit. He was also silenced by the Vatican for his teaching on religious freedom, separation of Church and state, and the way believers should participate in a democracy. Despite his official "silencing," he was brought to the Second Vatican Council as a personal advisor to the Archbishop of New York. His draft and writing became the Council's official text on "Religious Freedom." It has been called the single American contribution to the work of the Council. It represents an about face in the Church's understanding of personal freedom, political participation, and the rights of individuals to follow their conscience. It has strongly colored the thinking and practice of U.S. Catholics ever since.

Number 5 on my list is **Thomas Merton**, journalist, best-selling author and Trappist monk. He became the spiritual companion and mentor for millions of Americans when he published his dramatic autobiography, *The Seven Story Mountain*, exactly 50 years ago. As a monk and contemplative, he developed and promoted a spirituality of strong public ethics around issues, such as race relations, nonviolence, the war in Vietnam, and economic injustice. His sudden death in 1968 came as he was leading an international dialogue in Bangkok between Catholic monks and Eastern religious. For a great many, he embodied the quest for God and human solidarity in the modern world.

Number 6 on my list is a group of modern martyrs which include four American women who will always belong together: Maryknoll sisters **Moira Clarke** and **Ita Ford**, late, Ursuline sister **Dorothy Kegel**, and **Jean Donovan**, a lay missionary from Cleveland. They worked with the poor in El Salvador until they were murdered in 1980 by Salvadoran soldiers in civilian dress and "on special assignment." Their deaths had an enormous effect on the North American church, galvanizing opposition to US funding for the Salvadoran government. **Bishop Oscar Romero** had said, "It would be very sad if in a country where they are murdering the poor, there were no priests among the victims." In February, 1980, he asked President Carter to stop sending military aid to his government. On March 23rd, he appealed directly to the military of San Salvador, calling on them to disobey illegal orders to kill innocent people. On the next day, while he was saying Mass at the Carmelite Sisters' cancer hospital, a single rifle shot from the back of the chapel struck his heart and he was dead within minutes. In 1986, **six**

Jesuit professors who had called for a negotiated peace to stop the violence in their country were slain, along with two women (a housekeeper and her daughter), who had stayed with the Jesuits because they thought it would be safer there.

Number 7 on my list, **Cardinal Joseph Bernardin**, was Archbishop of Chicago at his death in 1996. He spent his earlier years bringing the U.S. bishops together around issues of nuclear peace, poverty in an affluent nation, and the "seamless garment" approach to the defense of life—linking opposition to abortion, to capital punishment and to euthanasia with social justice and a commitment to the poor. In his final years, he challenged Catholics in America to seek common ground and mutual respect, rather than divisiveness and in-fighting. Diagnosed with pancreatic cancer, he also (as his cover story in *Time* magazine reported) taught Americans how to face death. He said, "As a person of faith, I see death as a friend."

Number 8 on my list is **Mother Teresa of Calcutta**, who has been described as one of the most compelling Christian witnesses of the 20th century. She established centers and communities of service around the globe for the sick, the homeless, the dying, and the unwanted. It was not Mother Theresa's way to change social structures or take political action. "We are not social workers," she said, "but contemplatives in the heart of the world, for we are touching the Body of Christ twenty-four hours a day." When she was eventually "discovered" by the world press and honored by universities and a Nobel Peace Prize, she said, "We can do no great things, only small things with great love." And when people begged to travel to join her in her "wonderful work" in Calcutta, she told them sternly, "Find your own Calcutta!"

Number 9: When **Dorothy Day** died in 1980 at the age of 83, she was described as the most influential and significant figure in the history of the American Catholic Church. Earlier this month when a group of Catholic journalist and theologians voted on the most important Catholic lay person of the century,

Dorothy Day was their choice. As cofounder of the Catholic Worker movement, she represented a new kind of political holiness—a way of serving Christ both through prayer and care for the poor and also through solidarity with the poor in their struggle for justice. She combined traditional piety with St. Therese the Little Flower as her favorite saint, and radical social positions around pacifism (even during World War II), civil rights, and what she called "the mystery of the poor." "They are Jesus," she said, "and what you do to them, you do to Him."

Number 10: Last and, for me, the most significant figure on my list, is **Pope John XXIII.** You may recall his response to visitors at his first appearance as Pope who commented audibly, "My God, he's ugly." He answered, "Madam, I just won the papal election, not a beauty contest." John XXIII began a new era of openness to dialogue between all Christian churches and between the Church and the modern world. Beginning at age 77, and serving as Pope for only 5 years, he spoke of the need to "open the windows of the Church and let in fresh air." He called for *aggiornamento,* or updating, something that had been completely unheard of. The reform of the Mass, the Ecumenical movement, the teaching on religious freedom, and the stress on collegiality of bishops and the face and complexion of the Catholic Church as it enters the 21st century would be entirely different were it not for "good Pope John," who faced death in November of 1963 by saying, "My bags are packed, I'm ready to go."

On this feast of Epiphany, there is my list of the Wise Men and Women of our century and Church. For some it's like a history lesson, for others it's a chance to remember. For all of us, it's a time to give thanks for the variety of gifts and gifted people God brings into our lives.

Teilhard de Chardin

Homily of October 25, 2000

Unlike the Gospel according to Matthew or the Gospel according to Mark or the Gospel according to Luke, the Gospel according to John (1:1ff), that we just heard, does not begin on this planet. It begins beyond time and space, and it views Creation as coming forth from the wisdom and the word of God and finding its fulfillment in the light and glory of Jesus Christ. The Spiritual Star of the Millennium, whom I want to reflect on with you this morning, must have loved this passage very, very much.

Teilhard de Chardin was born in France in 1881. He was ordained a Jesuit priest in 1911. He served as a medic in the trenches of World War I. But, he was most noted and is most famous as a paleontologist (one who studies the ancient fossils of the earth) and as a theologian, and also as a scientist of the first rank, and as a visionary. Unlike many Church leaders before him, he did not grudgingly accept the findings of modern science or just barely justify the theory of evolution. He enthusiastically embraced it and recast it with a vision of Christian faith. He developed a philosophy in which sought to marry the science of the material world with the spiritual wisdom of the Church. You have to be honest that neither the scientific community nor the leaders of the Catholic Church were very quick to welcome his work. The scientific community felt that he was too much of a faithful believer to be that sound a scientist. And for Church leadership, he was too good and faithful a scientist to be a sound believer.

He spent from 1923 to 1946 on major excavations in Africa and China. He was among those who discovered the Peking Man, the earliest human remains found at that time. He published hundreds of well-received, scholarly articles about his research.

But his Jesuit superiors would not allow him to print anything on theology or his writings on religion and science. They were delighted that he was spending most of his time in Africa and out in China and not in the theological limelight of Europe. His writings were limited to circulation among a small circle of friends who were enthusiastic about him and supported him.

His fame grew enough that, for example, last evening, after our 5 o'clock Mass, one scientist came up to me and said, when he was studying in Berkeley in the early 1950s, he remembers the sensation it caused when Teilhard de Chardin arrived to give a lecture at UC Berkeley. The Vatican even put out a warning against his religious thoughts. That's enough notoriety, I guess.

His circle of friends was very small. When he died in New York City in 1955, on Easter Sunday, of all things (he had prayed to die on the Day of the Resurrection), only six people attended his funeral. And only one priest, only a single person, accompanied his remains to the cemetery. And they *misspelled his name* on the tombstone!

But, his friends immediately began publishing his works and, within five years (in 1960), this photo of him appeared in the Vatican pavilion at the World's Fair, where they bragged that he was "one of the greatest Christian thinkers of the twentieth century." Within ten years, his concepts and his vocabulary had woven their way into the official declarations of the Second Vatican Council. By then, his writings had inspired countless scholars, scientists and theologians throughout the world.

With many other scientists of his day, he rejected Darwin's Theory that what makes evolution work is the survival of the fittest. But, he went beyond those other critics. They settled with random chance and necessity as explanation enough. For Teilhard, *guided* chance and *guided* necessity drive the journey of the Universe. Then, he dared to ask the question, "If evolution is going somewhere and being led somewhere, who's leading it? And where is it going?"

Decades before the first time we got a view of our planet from outer space and long before satellites surrounded our globe, as well as cell phones and the internet and the World Wide Web, Teilhard de Chardin viewed our planet as becoming a "conscious global village," linked with conscious communication and a common destiny. He begins with the simplest elements, with rocks and stones and, even there, he finds the imprint of the energy and the imprint of a loving God. And, he goes on to a global vision of the Universe, where matter and spirit and body and soul and science and faith find their source in God and their unity in Christ.

His thinking is fairly complex. On Friday night, I'll be giving a summary of his teaching. Brian Swimme, a modern physicist, will be giving an update on the view of the Universe today. You may want to join us for that.

What lessons does Teilhard have for us today? I would say the first lesson is a warning. That we have to be able to listen to one another and learn. Listen critically, but learn. What a loss that he was never able to share his thoughts with anyone during his lifetime, so that he could listen to and refine his thoughts. And the world wasn't able to listen to him and dialog with him. We have to be willing to listen and learn, but beyond those lessons of warning, there are gifts from him.

To me, the first gift from Teilhard is the realization that I do not live in a two-room house or in a two-story universe. I don't live in a house where in one room I have everything I find out from science. Then, there's a wall and a locked door. In the other room is everything I find out from faith. On one story the natural, on the other the supernatural. One place where God is and the other place where God ain't. Instead, science and faith welcome and enrich one another. I live in a one-room house. In the same way, I don't live in a two-story universe, where in one story we have the matter and in the other we have spirit. We live in a Universe where God is truly present, the Word made flesh. We live in a world of spirit and flesh at the same time, all around us.

Teilhard also reminds us that we should value the work of our hands and the relationships of our hearts, because they are not passing and perishable. They have a communal and cosmic future. Another way of putting it is, God takes our lives and who we are and what we do very seriously. It's going somewhere. And finally, Teilhard reminds us of the poetry of another Jesuit (remember that phrase, "The world is charged with the grandeur of God"?). He reminds us that that is not just poetry. It's not a metaphor. It's not romantic thought. Rather, it is an accurate description of how near our God is, at work in our Universe, on our Earth, in our flesh, and in our lives, bringing forth and building up the Kingdom of God at every moment.

Let us give thanks to the Lord Who is so good. Amen.

Prayer for the Grace to Age Well

When the signs of age begin to mark my body
(and still more when they touch my mind);
when illness that is to diminish me or carry me off
strikes from without or is born within me;
when the painful moment comes to which I suddenly awaken
to the fact that I am growing ill or growing old:
and above all at the last moment
when I feel I am losing hold of myself
and am absolutely passive within the hands
of the great unknown forces that have formed me;
in all these dark moments, O God,
grant that I may understand that it is you
(provided only my faith is strong enough)
who are painfully parting the fibers of my being
in order to penetrate to the very marrow
of my substance and bear me away within yourself.

Pierre Teilhard
de Chardin. S.J.

FATHER JOYCE RETIRES

by Alfred J. Garrotto
Special to *The Catholic Voice*

As he embarks on his well-deserved retirement, Oakland native Rev. Brian T. Joyce can look back on a life dedicated to the growth and spiritual well-being of our diocese.

For 26 years as pastor, Father Joyce has guided Christ the King Parish in Pleasant Hill along the principles of the Gospel and Second Vatican Council.

Many Christ the King parishioners have grown up during Father Joyce's quarter-century as their pastor. He has married them, baptized their children and buried their dead. Many admit to mixed emotions as he enters retirement.

He entered St. Joseph Seminary in Mountain View at the age of 12 and was ordained to the priesthood in 1963 at St. Anthony Church in East Oakland. For the past 51 years, the Oakland diocese has been his home and his field of ministry.

Father Joyce began his ministry as associate pastor of St. Lawrence O'Toole Parish, followed by four years as associate at St. Augustine Parish. In 1967, Bishop Floyd L. Begin named him diocesan Director of Adult Education. From 1970-1979, he served as chancellor of the diocese, under Bishop Begin and Bishop John S. Cummins.

After Father Joyce's tenure as chancellor, Bishop Cummins appointed him pastor of St. Monica Parish. For the next 10 years, the Moraga community became a model of St. Pope John XIII's vision for a welcoming, warm and loving parish life. In 1988, he succeeded the much beloved Msgr. James J. Wade as pastor of Christ the King Parish, Pleasant Hill. He also lent his wisdom and discernment to the clergy personnel board for 22 years. In addition, he formed the Diocesan Pastoral Council and served as consultant and writer on the Bishop's National Committee for Priestly Life in Ministry.

According to parish council member Carol Vogl, "We'll miss Father Brian's guidance and openness. At the same time, we see this as the right time for him to lessen the burdens of leading such an active community."

Other parishioners wonder what they will do without him. All will miss his personal touch, his sense of humor, and his truly caring and listening manner.

Father Joyce's ground-up leadership style allowed parishioners to engage in new and innovative ministries that now total 60, most of them lay-created and led. Parishioners have been especially grateful for his emphasis on adult education that inspired Catholic adults to become "adult Catholics."

Father Joyce shared personal memories of his life and ministry:

What will you miss most about pastoring a thriving parish?

The people in our parish have been willing to participate, provide leadership, and speak up. Because of that, we've had a consistently good liturgical experience, a concrete commitment to social justice, and high quality adult education. I'm going to miss being an active part of all that.

What won't you miss about parish ministry?

I won't miss the busyness of administration. I love it, but it has drained my energy. Leadership in the Church requires listening to people's concerns, being open to change and being decisive in setting a direction for the community. It troubled me that, because of administrative commitments, I never had enough time to spend with people, bond with them, and follow up on their needs after meeting with them.

What are your memories of being chancellor?

I saw my role as one of encouraging healthy practices in parishes and enabling people in the diocese to achieve what was best for themselves and the Church. But, I spent most of my time shutting down unhealthy practices. I decided I could make a more positive impact as a parish priest. As pastor, I had greater influence in making good things happen for people.

Your career covered some turbulent decades in Church history. Some priests chose to leave the ministry. What was that era like for you, and why did you choose to stay in the priesthood?

It was heartbreaking to see some of the best priests and good friends resign. In another sense, I saw it as a time for challenge and growth for the Church. Their resignation was a conscientious response to the teachings of the Gospel and Vatican II. At the same time, the Church needed clergy who were faithful to the Council and fostered openness and free discussion of all things Catholic. I was committed to that new vision and felt called to remain an active part of the Church.

You have sometimes been criticized—even called "notorious"—by fellow Catholics, who disagreed with your leadership style. How have you dealt with that?

I took that criticism as a compliment. It represented so few Catholics and none of our own parishioners. Critics opposed me for following the teachings of the Gospel and the lead of Vatican II. I applied both of these at the diocesan and parish levels. In my view, my critics have been out of touch with the Gospel vision of a Church that is open and inclusive, fostering community and promoting justice and equal rights for all people.

Your parishioners have a reputation for being "noisy" in church. How do you respond to that?

I dislike the notion of a "silent" church. It scares me. Silence builds barriers. I don't think Jesus and the Gospels call us to create barriers. Rather, they call us to gather in his name and 'celebrate' our worship. There is always a place for reverence and silence — reverence to the presence of Christ in the tabernacle and silence for prayer and meditation. I've tried to find ways to greet people and welcome them, while leaving space for privacy and quiet meditation.

What accomplishments are you most proud of?

I'd say I'm most proud of building lively parishes of welcome, in which people worship well, fully participate, and answer the call to engage in ministries — both traditional and innovative. I did my best to foster that kind of lay leadership and participation.

Father Joyce plans to take up residence in Alameda, where he can keep closer tabs on his beloved Oakland Raiders.

Mary Joyce and Brian Joyce early on.

Young Seminarian.

Director of Adult Education.

Class of 1963 at a much later date.

Chorus boys in *Bye, Bye Birdie! (left to right)* Fr. Brian Joyce, Fr. Jerry Kennedy, Fr. Ralph Brennan, Fr. Ed Haasl with Gloria Manning.

Thirteen priests dance in *Hello Dolly, (left to right)* Msgr. Maurovitch, Fr. Ralph Brennan, Fr. Don Hudson, Fr. Ed Haasl, Fr. Don Osuna, Fr. Joe Carroll, myself, Fr. Jim O'Connor, Fr. Jerry Kennedy, Fr. John Maxwell, Fr. Bob Ponciroli, Fr. Jim Erickson, Fr. Paul Vassar with Rosemary Thomas.

The Rev. Brian Joyce of Christ the King Catholic Church in Pleasant Hill says worshipers switching churches is better than abandoning religion altogether. "Today," he said, "a growing number of people say, 'What parish meets my needs?'" *The Sunday Times, Sept. 21, 1997*

Outdoor Mass.

Myself advising Pope John Paul II.

Greeting people at Retirement Mass.

William McGarvey, Executive Director of Interfaith Council of Contra Costa, presents a "Making a Difference Award" at my Retirement Mass.

Priests concelebrating at my Retirement Mass: *(left to right)* Fr. Paul Schmidt, Fr. Hermon Leong, Fr. Padraig Greene, Fr. Tom Burns, Fr. Dan Danielson, Fr. Larry Young, Fr. Richard Mangini, Fr. Paul Vassar, and Fr. Jayson Landeza.

Retirement Mass with *(left to right)* Fr. Dan Derry, parish Deacon, John Ashmore, myself, and Fr. Dan Danielson.

Bishop Barber "Greets me" at Retirement Mass.

Bishop John Cummins speaks at my Retirement Mass.

SUBSTANTIAL . . .

The second grouping of items I describe as *Substantial*. Actually, most of these items come from what I consider the basis for anything substantial in the Church today, which is the teaching and priorities of Vatican Council II. Most of these items come from my "Four-Minute Specials." Inspired by Bishop Ken Untener of Saginaw, MI, and begun at Christ the King by myself in 2002. I begin with Vatican II itself and then a lot of issues and fall-out that follow from the presence of Jesus in the Eucharist to whatever happened to Original Sin, Limbo and Purgatory. I include everything from comments on prayer and adult education to the role of Pope Francis today and the perennial issue, "Why Go to Mass?"

The Second Vatican Council and the Year of Faith (I)

Bulletin Letter — October 7, 2012

Beginning this week, Catholics throughout the world have been invited to observe a Year of Faith. This has been called for by Pope Benedict XVI to begin on October 11th of this year and to continue until the Feast of Christ the King in November 2013. My first reaction is, "Well and good, but what good does that do?" Didn't we have a Year of the Family in the 1980s, and what about the Year of the Priests in 2009? I also recall that Pope Paul VI declared a Year of Faith in 1967. Did any of those make a difference? No one really imagines that a Year of Faith eradicates decades of skepticism, doubt, unbelief and indifference, and anyway aren't we all called to be people who work at our faith every year of our lives—not just 2012-2013?

However, two things do give me hope. First of all, the Pope has deliberately chosen October 11th, the 50th anniversary of the opening of the Second Vatican Council, as the start-up date for the Year of Faith. The spirit and direction of Vatican II is always a source of hope that is well worth remembering. Secondly, if we could each do at least one thing new and different during the Year of Faith for our study, reflection, or prayer life that might make a difference well worth the time and effort.

The Second Vatican Council, which took place between 1962 and 1965, is easily the most significant event in the previous 100 years of the Church's history. Some would argue that it was the most significant event in the 2000 years of Christianity! At the local parish level, it meant that we would begin to worship in English rather than Latin and be urged to become active participants rather than silent observers. It signaled enormous changes in the life of the Church, but first and foremost that change itself is necessary and possible. It also underlined the importance of Scripture for Catholics. It changed our attitude towards relationships with other religions and the world around us and called for religious freedom. Perhaps the number-one shift in understanding the Church, one we are still trying to work out in practice, is that the Church is not "those guys" (popes and bishops), but really all of us, called by the Council "The People of God." The Second Vatican Council also put at the top of our consciousness the primacy of individual conscience. It says that all are bound to follow their conscience faithfully and that true religion consists, before anything else, internal, voluntary and free choices. Much of this we take for granted as ordinary and obvious, but before the Second Vatican Council, it was not ordinary or obvious at all. That is why I think of the spirit and direction of Vatican II as such a source of hope and so well worth remembering.

We begin the Year of Faith this coming Thursday, October 11th with "Vatican II: Celebrating Fifty Years Ago and Fifty Years After," the first of two nights of Adult Ed, here in Church at 7:30 p.m. My suggestion to do "one thing new and different" during the Year of Faith could be simply to attend one of the Adult Ed sessions for the first time. For those for whom nighttime sessions are not practical, the daytime program, "Enneagram and the Bible," meets Tuesdays from 9-11 a.m. in the Parish Hall (October 9, 16, 23, & 30). Another "at least one thing new and different" could be to add to your prayer life one prayer about the Year of Faith every day. I suggest cutting out the official prayer printed in today's foldout and using it every day in the year ahead.

Prayer in Celebration of the
50th Anniversary of the Opening of Vatican Council II

Eternal God, you called your Church at the Second Vatican
Council to stir into flame afresh the riches of grace that
abide in her heart, and bid us seek from you a new and fiery
Pentecost. In fidelity to this call,
sanctify your Church by a new outpouring of the Holy Spirit,
that we might set the world ablaze with the liberating truth
and radiant beauty of your beloved Son, Jesus Christ;
for you, O Father, are the
lover of mankind. Amen.

Prayer Courtesy T. Neal © 2012
www.CatholicYearofFaith.com   Card#YOF-3

The Second Vatican Council (II)

Bulletin Letter — March 11, 2012

Thank you for your response to the "parishioner survey" we
asked for in January and early February. Our Parish Council
is busy collating and analyzing the results. Currently, we have
received 811 responses! I'll give you a summary of the results
as soon as possible. Meanwhile, the Parish council will be
compiling, analyzing, and organizing an evaluation, and they
will be contacting all the respondents whenever possible and
appropriate.

At the same time we continue to remember and celebrate
the 50th Anniversary of the Second Vatican Council (1962-1965).
This weekend we focus on the "call to worship well."

Among the distinctive teachings of Vatican II, by contrast
with some common beliefs of the pre-Vatican II era, are the
following:

1. The Church is, first and foremost, a mystery, or sacrament,
   and not primarily an organization or institution.
2. The Church is the whole People of God, not just the
   hierarchy, clergy, and religious.
3. The Church's mission includes action on behalf of justice
   and peace and is not limited to the preaching of the Word
   and the celebration of the Sacraments.
4. The Church includes all Christians and is not limited
   exclusively to the Catholic Church.
5. The Church is a communion, or college, of local churches,
   which are not simply administrative subdivisions or mere
   branches of the Church universal.
6. The lay apostolate is a direct participation in the mission of
   the Church and not simply a sharing in the mission of the
   hierarchy.

7. God uses other Christian churches and non-Christian religions in offering salvation to all humankind; the Catholic Church is not the only means of salvation.
8. The dignity of the human person and the freedom of the act of faith are the foundation of religious liberty for all, over against the older view that "error has no rights."
9. We have the right to act in conscience and in freedom, so as to personally make moral decisions. "We must not be forced to act contrary to our conscience. Nor must we be prevented from acting according to our conscience, especially in religious matters."
10. "Liturgies which are meant to be celebrated in common, with the faithful present and actively participating, should as far as possible be celebrated in that way rather than by an individual and quasi-privately."

The Second Vatican Council (III)

4-Minute Special Homily — March 4, 2001

Before the collection and the final announcements and the final blessing, we're going to have the first of our four-minute specials or, as people on sports radio might call it, four-minute drills. In a moment when I start, you can watch me and your watch at the same time. See if I keep to the time.

The topic today is "The Second Vatican Council" or "Vatican II." There is a writer who says there are three groups who go to Catholic Churches today: Pre-Council people (before Vatican II), Post-Council people (after Vatican II), and the vast majority who are the "'What-Council?'-People.' Vatican II was a gathering of 2,600 bishops, convened by the Pope, that met from 1962 to 1965. It produced sixteen documents to fashion our best understanding of our Catholic tradition and our Christian faith and its best direction for today and for the years to come.

One question might be: How important is that Council? You can answer it by asking another question. In the Roman Catholic Church, what is the highest authority? Now, all of us know that the correct answer is the pastor!! Or, at least, all of us pastors know that. The media and a lot of people say the Pope is the highest authority in the Roman Catholic Church. But, that is not accurate. In the Catholic tradition, the highest authority is a General Council invoked, not always but most of the time, by the Pope to address the issues of the Church.

Probably the greatest Catholic theologian of the 20th century was Karl Rahner. And he said, "In 2,000 years, the three most important events in the life of Christianity were the Council of Jerusalem that decided Gentiles could be baptized without becoming Jews, the Council of Trent that fashioned our Latin Mass with the back to the people and our attitude toward Protestant Christians (which was defensive and hostile, and they immediately returned the favor!), and thirdly, one that took place in our lifetime, the 21st of the General Councils, the Second Vatican Council that took place in Rome in 1962-1965." What did it decide?

We know it set the revision of our liturgy by calling for our own language and active participation of everyone. It underlined the importance of Scripture for Catholics, changed our attitude toward relationships with other religions and with the world around us, and called for religious freedom.

If I were to underline two things that were most important from the Council, the first was recovering who the Church is by saying that the Church is not as we had slipped into believing (that it is the hierarchy, the bishops, the religious, and the clergy), but the Church is the people of God, all of us. What has happened since the Council is that we have been struggling and will continue to search for authentic ways to change our behavior and put into practice the reality that we are the Church.

And the second most important thing I would list is that the Council recovered the importance and primacy of individual conscience. This was hidden in our theology books all along. It was even tucked into the *Baltimore Catechism*. But most of us didn't hear much about it growing up. The Second Vatican Council put at the top of our consciousness and at the top of the shelf the primacy of individual conscience. It said that all are bound to follow their conscience faithfully and that true religion consists, before everything else, in internal, voluntary, free, *free*, *free* choices. Now, that has caused a lot of confusion and growth in our Church since 1965. First of all, it calls for freedom from all external pressure and force when people make decisions. It also calls that internally we are bound to seek the truth as honestly and as best as we possibly can.

So if anyone asks you, "Do you know what Vatican II is?", your answer now is, "I do."

What Ever Happened to Original Sin?

4-Minute Special Homily — March 17, 2002

Whatever happened to Original Sin? When I was in the fourth grade, I knew all about Original Sin. Adam and Eve had disobeyed and that really irritated God (Whom, I was told, gets upset very easily). God immediately threw them out of the Garden of Eden and made the rest of us pay the price by locking the gates of heaven and leaving the stain of Original Sin on each one of us. Only Christ could unlock the gates, and only Baptism could remove the stain.

Original Sin is quite real, but it is something very different from that Fourth Grade version. At one level, you don't even need the Church, the Bible, or faith to know about Original Sin. Just read the daily newspaper. This world is a dangerous place, not very safe to grow up in, and with more than enough evil to go around. Add to that, every one of us has a dark side. Left to our own devices, there is a serious question whether we can be fully trusted. We seem to be quite prone to sin. Some would attribute this to the whole evolutionary process, which was survival of the fittest, me-first, natural selection, and self-survival that got us this far in the first place.

Whatever the source, the kind of compassion and selfless love needed to fulfill God's gracious promise of lasting life doesn't seem to come easily to any of us. On the other hand, Christ invites us to a new way of life. The Bible, which talks about Original Sin, not in Genesis with Adam and Eve, but in the New Testament with Christ, tells us that, just as sin has entered the human race and is universal, so the reconciling victory of Jesus is even more powerful and universal.

The significance of Baptism is that if we are plunged (baptized) into a community of brothers and sisters who work at proclaiming God's love and living by Christ's Gospel and Spirit, then the world becomes a safer place for us, and we ourselves can be transformed. The upside-down, backwards way of saying that is, "Baptism takes away Original Sin."

One other thing that was not so clear to me back in the Fourth Grade was that, while life in a community of baptized believers may promise a safer world and a better "Brian," the struggle doesn't end there. Original Sin still has a way of hanging around. Our universe, the human condition, and our personal journey are still unfinished. We have a long way to go! Wherever the in-dwelling of God's Holy Spirit is absent from our lives, Original Sin still casts its shadow. We are born falling short of God's promise into a world where the accumulation of evil limits our freedom and threatens our future.

What happened to Original Sin? It's still very much alive and well. (Just read the papers!) But at the same time, Christ has brought God's saving wisdom and life-giving Spirit to our world. In fact, St. Paul says, "To our entire universe." And Christ is not just alive and well, but His risen Spirit is much more powerful by far than Original Sin. And that's good news . . . very good news indeed!

Baptism and Misconceptions

4-Minute Special Homily — May 26, 2002

The feast of the Holy Trinity is not a bad day to reflect on our Baptisms. In four minutes, let me share three misconceptions about Baptism.

Misconception #1 is that Baptism is for and about babies. That's a fairly common opinion since many of us were baptized as babies, most of us have gone to babies' baptisms, and all of us remember the famous shootout in the movie, "The Godfather," which takes place during a baby's baptism. Despite the large number of infants baptized into the Christian family, Baptism is really about adults and an adult process which demands study, faith, discernment and a mature decision. Adult baptism, and the journey that precedes it, is the norm and standard in the Catholic community. Only by exception do we baptize infants and only on the presumption that the family is seriously Christian and the child will be led through the steps of study, faith, discernment, and mature decision as she/he grows up in that committed family.

Misconception #2 is that baptism is about getting rid of Original Sin. There is some truth to that, but the misconception is that we've got it exactly backwards. The primary purpose of Baptism is not to scrub us clean of some sin (original or not) but entry into the community of believers and witnesses to the message, person, and life of Jesus Christ. It is not the sacrament of removal, but the sacrament of *belonging*. One great side effect of moving into a community that takes responsibility for passing on the wisdom and life-giving presence of Jesus is that it uproots and protects us from that fallen and fragile condition theologians call Original Sin and gives us greater freedom from a world of darkness and the bonds of sin.

Misconception #3 is that Baptism gives us no more than an entry level position, a bottom rung location, a private first-class rank in the Church, the Body of Christ. The real members, the really important promotion, the big positions come with religious orders, ordination, and ecclesiastical honors, you know, nuns and priests, monsignors and bishops, cardinals and popes! The Catholic Christian conviction about Baptism is just the opposite!

When we are baptized into the Church and Body of Christ there can be no greater dignity and responsibility. Every baptized Christian is already called and promoted to be an active, co-responsible member of the Church with a unique, distinctive contribution to make. It is that rather recent rediscovery of the dignity of Baptism that has led to religious returning to their baptismal names, rather than using the less important name taken when they became nuns, brothers, or priests and to the growing custom of young people retaining their baptismal name when they are confirmed. It has led to the active participation of laity in the ministries of worship and of finance, planning and decision-making committees for parishes and diocese. It has even led to standing tall rather than kneeling for communion and reaching out with baptized hands to receive the host rather than being fed as inferior children. One prominent theologian and scholar of Church history has said that, while the Church today features dozens of schools of spirituality, the New Testament and early Church knew of one approach and one only. Simply put, it was "Christian, remember who you are; Christian, remember your Baptism."

The Real Presence of Jesus in the Entire Eucharist

4-Minute Special Homily — June 9, 2002

This weekend: four minutes about the real presence of Jesus—not in Communion, but a communion. A funny thing happened to Catholics on their way to Mass. Once upon a time, Catholic Christians at Eucharist, as the New Testament tells us, recognized that Christ was among them as they gathered in His name. They passed on precious words of Scripture knowing it was a living contact with the person of Jesus. They recognized Him in the breaking of the bread and celebrated that they were one body with Him, just as they shared one bread and one cup.

Somewhere in the Dark and Middle Ages, Catholics' attention became almost completely riveted on the host, and whether out of awe or out of superstition, or no longer understanding the Latin, or a sense of unworthiness, they seldom received communion, but came mainly to watch the host and the chalice held up high. Then in the 1500s, Catholics understood (or in some cases, misunderstood) Protestant reformers to say that Jesus was not really present in Communion, but it was just a symbolic reminder of Him. That really got their dander up. As Catholics went to Mass, they insisted and focused on one thing to the exclusion of everything else, namely, that the Mass produces the real presence of Christ in the consecrated bread and wine, and nothing else compares to that or even matters much. A funny thing had happened to Catholics on the way to Mass; they forgot their own faith in the presence of Christ in the entire celebration of the Eucharist, and in many ways beyond the Mass.

This Eucharistic amnesia led to some strange behavior and consequences. Even though it is Catholic faith that Christ is present as we assemble in His name, and that He is present even as we hear the word of Scripture proclaimed, they were told it's really OK if you miss the entire first part of the Mass—the gathering, and the Liturgy of the Word. Just be sure to get in before the really important things begin to happen (you know, like the collection). Hopefully, we've moved well beyond that as the Second Vatican Council (way back in the 1960s) spoke of Christ's presence not only in consecrated bread and wine but also in the proclaimed Word and the assembly itself. As one of our official Eucharistic prayers reads: "Blessed too is Your son, Jesus Christ, who is present among us and whose love gathers us together. As once He did for His disciples, Christ now opens the Scriptures for us and breaks the bread."

Pope Paul VI, in his encyclical letter on the Eucharist, reaffirmed belief in the presence of Christ in Communion. He also spoke of the very real presence of Christ in acts of concern and compassion, in the preaching of God's Word, in the faithful shepherding of God's people, and in the celebration of all the sacraments. Christ comes to us in many ways, but the Mass (not one magic moment, but the Mass from beginning to end) is the principal and most important way He touches us, nourishes us, calls and causes us to be His body and sends us out to make a difference in our world.

The Real Presence of Jesus in the Bread and Wine

4-Minute Special Homily — June 2, 2002

This weekend, we'll have four minutes about the real presence of Jesus in the consecrated bread and wine of Communion. Next weekend's four minutes will be about the real presence of Jesus in the entire Mass. Having those two separate topics may in itself be surprising news to a lot of Catholics, because the signature of Roman Catholic belief has been so identified with Christ being really present in Communion that the rest of Catholic belief about the other ways Christ is present often gets overlooked, forgotten and ignored.

The Catholic belief and conviction about the real presence of Jesus in Communion finds its foundation in our faith that the Risen Lord is no longer bound by the particular restraints of time and place. However, that belief stands midway between two extremes which the Church has always rejected.

The first extreme which the Church rejects is the understanding that Christ's presence is "merely symbolic" and no more than that, that Communion serves simply as a reminder of the life, death and love of Jesus, that the bread of Communion keeps us from forgetting Him. So the presence of Jesus, if anything, is all in our heads or in our remembering. A second and quite different extreme which the Church also rejects is the view that Jesus is physically present, that is, present *materially*, so that somehow His atoms and molecules hide just beneath the surface of the bread and wine. Sometimes our own vocabulary, with words like "real presence," "substantial presence," and even "physical presence," betrays us into this extreme. Both extremes, "symbolic" and "material," misrepresent scripture, tradition and orthodox Catholic belief.

The authentic Catholic understanding about Christ's presence in Communion can be described in two statements:

1) The presence of Jesus is personal and it is real. It is not the presence of an object or thing, but the personal presence of the Lord. The old *Baltimore Catechism* and its answer that Christ is present, "Body and Blood, Soul and Divinity" was trying to get at that whole personal presence. 2) It is the presence of the Risen and Spirit-filled Christ, not a matter of molecular flesh and body fluids. Christ's Aramaic words at the Last Supper, "This is My body; This is My blood," are more helpfully and accurately put into English as, "This is Myself, and this is My life given for you." The traditional Catholic teaching about "transubstantiation" has been a way of protecting belief in the substantial, personal presence of Christ and, at the same time, excluding belief in a material physical or molecular change in bread and wine. That's the "what" of Communion. How about the "why?"

Through the centuries from New Testament days, the Church has recognized that the "why," the fundamental purpose of Christ's presence, is not for Him to be adored and not for our isolated private devotion and piety. The goal and purpose of Christ's presence is to lead us as a body in a sacrifice of praise to God, our Creator, Father and Author. Its further purpose is to nourish our lives and to transform us into the community of His body and to empower that body, a Eucharistic people, to continue His mission. Communion is important and vital to who we are and to what we must become. But, so is the presence of Christ in many other ways.

What Ever Happened to Limbo?

4-Minute Special Homily — November 11, 2001

"Whatever happened to Limbo?"

The 4-minute special is back—so check your watches and keep me honest!

This weekend's topic is, "Whatever happened to Limbo?" Here's the short answer: while Purgatory (with a very different feel and a thoroughly revised understanding) remains very much a part of Catholic teaching and belief, Limbo does not. Just check out the new, official *Catholic Catechism*. It has 2,865 paragraphs. Purgatory gets three paragraphs, Limbo zero—not even a mention!

While the phrase to be "stuck in limbo" has become part of the English language, the theory of Limbo is linked in Church history to the question, "What happens to unbaptized babies when they die?" Given the teaching that baptism is necessary for salvation, what becomes of them and, for that matter, what happens to good adults who led good lives but without faith or baptism? The earliest church theologian to address that question had a brief and brutal answer. St. Augustine, who lived in the early 400s, taught that they are all in hell, but in a corner of hell where the flames are not at their highest. (Thanks a lot Augustine!) Catholic theologians in the Middle Ages revised and softened that answer by developing a theory that there must be a place on the border or on the threshold between heaven and hell. The Latin word for border or threshold is *limbo*! These unbaptized infants and non-believing but very good grownups enjoy natural happiness but don't ever get home to be with God. Some have likened it to a celestial and eternal day care center (thanks a lot, one *more* time!).

Five points describe the Church's attitude today toward Limbo (when and if the subject ever comes up):

1. All this talk about Limbo was strictly a theory proposed and discussed by theologians in a day and age when people's reaction was "that sounds pretty reasonable to me." Today, people's reaction, including theologians, is quite the opposite.

2. At no time was this theory proposed or defined as official church teaching or Christian belief (although many of our grade school teachers from years ago would be very surprised to hear that, and they certainly didn't tell me).

3. The theory of Limbo was based on a fundamentalist, literalist and mistaken interpretation of Christ's words on the necessity of baptism. This interpretation took "unless a man is born again of water and the spirit he cannot enter the kingdom of God" as restricting God and refusing God permission to be loving, saving, and forgiving, no matter what the circumstance.

4. It ignored a much more basic and central Catholic belief that God wills the salvation of every human being. Remember the *Baltimore Catechism*: "God made us to know him, love him and serve him in this world and to be happy with him in the next."

5. The theory of Limbo missed the Bible's most direct answer to the fate of unbaptized infants who die. "'Even if a mother forget her unborn child, I will not forget you,' says the Lord" (Isaiah 49:15, paraphrased). There's the best answer.

Limbo, or what someone once called "a workable solution to a sticky problem," is not workable, nor it is a solution, nor is it credible.

And that's what's happened to Limbo, or as Fr Dibble might say, "Forget about it!"

Where Is Pope Francis?

Bulletin Letter — September 22, 2013

Where is Pope Francis? The easiest and most common answer to that has got to be, "He's in his car, he's on the phone, he's in dialogue with non-believers, and he's very concerned about Syria."

He's in his car. From all reports, Pope Francis is enjoying being Pope, but he doesn't like the restrictions to his movement and having to be escorted everywhere. A few weeks ago he was given a "new" car, a 1984 Renault with 186,000 miles on it. As one paper reported it, his "Popemobile" is a lot like himself, "frugal, all in white, and with a fair bit of mileage." A visiting seventy-year-old priest gave the Pope his old car, which he had used for years to visit the poor and the needy. When the priest told him that half of the people who came with him were stuck outside the Vatican gates because of security, the Pope grabbed the keys and said, "Let's go," driving stick shift and all.

He's on the phone. Pope Francis is both unnerving the Vatican and delighting the faithful by spontaneously picking up the phone and calling people, earning the nickname, "The Cold-Call Pope." This month he called to comfort a pregnant woman whose married boyfriend had tried to pressure her to have an abortion. The Pope offered to personally baptize the baby when it is born next year. He called another man who had written to the Pope after a series of tragedies in his family, most recently the killing of his brother in a robbery. The Pope said that the letter had made him cry. Some Vatican analysts fear that papal phone calls will create disillusion among those not getting a call (he hasn't called me, has he called you?). And others fear that many, including the press, will be deceived by hoaxes.

He's in dialogue with non-believers. Recently, the Pope has written to make three points. 1) God has never abandoned his covenant with the Jewish people, and the Church can never be grateful enough to the Jews for preserving their faith despite the horrors of history; 2) God's mercy does not have limits and reaches to nonbelievers, for whom sin will not be the lack of faith in God, but failure to follow their own consciences; 3) Truth is not variable or subjective, but is always expressed in accordance with someone's history, culture and the situation in which they live.

He's concerned about Syria. Recently Pope Francis called for a special day of prayer and fasting as part of a full-court press against military intervention against Syria. He also wrote to Russian President Putin to insist that a military solution in Syria will be futile. He forcefully declared that "violence and war are never the way to peace" and that "forgiveness, dialogue, reconciliation—these are the ways of peace in beloved Syria, in the Middle East, and in all the world."

Advising the Pope!

Purgatory

Bulletin Letter — November 11, 2012

It doesn't happen too often, but this week Broadway comes to Pleasant Hill. I first saw the play *Doubt* back in 2004 on Broadway. Next Friday, it will be presented right here in Pleasant Hill in our own parish church. My best remembrance, aside from greatly enjoying the play, was that the tickets cost about $50 at that time. Broadway plays now run between $100-$300 per ticket. Here at Christ the King the play, quite professionally done, will be nearby and available for a donation of $10. Such a deal! Don't miss it!

The month of November is a special time when we remember "Our Beloved Dead," beginning with All Souls Day (November 2nd), our Bereavement Mass, and the annual celebration at the graves of Msgr. Wade, Margo Schorno, and Fr. Declan Deane. It continues up to Thanksgiving and the Feast of Christ the King. For many of us, it is a time to pray for "those in Purgatory."

For those of us from an older generation, the question we may be asking is, "Whatever happened to Purgatory?" Those from a younger generation may be asking, "What's Purgatory?!" Purgatory is the Catholic Christian belief that affirms a transitional spiritual stage after death that, if it's necessary, gets us ready for the fullness of God's presence and kingdom.

When I was growing up, the general opinion was that, when we die, most of us won't be bad enough to go to hell or good enough to get into heaven, so Purgatory provides a space to work out the rough edges and serves as a kind of "Catholic safety net" or "Christian finishing school." We would pray regularly to help our deceased friends and relatives to graduate quickly.

Now here's what's happened to our belief in Purgatory. Not all, but a great many Catholics have figured out that while the basic belief in the need to be made ready to meet our God is rooted in both scripture and common sense, our way of imagining Purgatory, our descriptions, our images, and much of our way of thinking about Purgatory does not come from our faith or from our Church teaching but from poets like Dante and artists like Michelangelo, who with their dramatic and medieval flair gave us the image of having to "do time" in a fiery prison, and the impression of our God acting like a punitive warden, rather than the loving God revealed by Jesus.

When it comes to that final "getting ready" which is really accomplished by the loving grace of God, the new Catholic Catechism was careful to remove any dramatic descriptions and even deleted the word "painful" from its original draft. When it comes to the amount of time to be spent in detention, many modern scholars suggest that our Purgatory, or getting ready, may well be instantaneous, or that it coincides with the moment of death.

But, have you noticed we Catholics still pray for the dead? Why is that? I don't think it's to get our loved ones an early pardon from purgatory or to help them escape from a divine "lock up." Here are four reasons:

1. Praying for the dead is a Catholic way of saying that their life goes on; there's more!
2. Praying for the dead witnesses to a communion and solidarity—that we continue to gently hold on to one another by faith and by prayer, even after death;
3. Praying for the dead is both a human and Christian way of saying, "We do not forget." Or better, "We will not forget."
4. If our day-to-day experience of life is any indication, whether before or after death, there is constant change, growth, ongoing dynamic blossoming. So, we pray that our loved ones may continue to grow and to advance in bliss and in joy until one day, with their rough edges gone and our rough edges made smooth, we will all meet again.

Our belief in Purgatory and prayer for the dead remains constant. But, for most of us, our feeling for and understanding of Purgatory has changed a great deal. That's what's happened to Purgatory.

Prayer

Bulletin Letter — July 1, 2012

Our community has recently suffered a major loss, as Rev. Brian Stein-Webber, Director of the Interfaith Council of Contra Costa County for the last six years, has resigned to accept a major position at the Lutheran Theological Seminary. Among the many outstanding services Brian has constantly provided to us was his monthly newsletter, "Ministering Together," which usually included bulletin items from other pastors under, "Your Words." Here is one I especially like by Rev. Ron Dunn of San Ramon Valley United Methodist Church. Ron calls it "The Answer of Unanswered Prayer: A Personal Point of View." He begins it with a quote from Garth Brooks *"I thank God for unanswered prayer."* Here it is in its entirety:

> *I grew up listening to the late Bill King broadcast Warrior basketball games on the radio. King, of course, had his own unique way of making the fast-paced action of a game come alive within his listener's imagination. Although we were only listening to his rapid-fire verbal descriptions, it was almost as if we were sitting courtside and watching the game unfold. One of my favorite Bill King descriptions was when Rick Barry would get the ball and King would describe the unfolding drama...*
>
> *Barry with the ball, drives the baseline...*
> *Shot clock running down...*
> *can't find anyone open...*
> *throws up a prayer...*
> *(pregnant pause)...*
> *ANSWERED!*

It was vintage Bill King—even if his understanding of the nature of prayer might be a little suspect. Is that, after all, really the way prayer works? Is it really a matter of launching a heaven-bound request and then holding our breath as we wait to see if our request is answered? While some are inclined to see it that way, I am not so sure. You see, that particular understanding of prayer tends to assume that the "answer" to prayer is to get whatever it is that you are praying for— whether it's a winning basket, a high test score, or a promotion at work.

While this approach may seem to work for us in certain situations, it will ultimately prove to be hugely disappointing, for, inevitably, we will encounter those situations when the ball glances off the rim, the test score is below average, and the promotion goes to someone else. What happens then to our theology of prayer? Do we conclude that our prayer failed? Do we begin to suspect that prayer simply doesn't work?

That might well be the case—if our understanding of prayer is predicated upon getting only the results that we want. But, if we learn to understand that the purpose of prayer is NOT about getting what we want, but about getting what we need, we might begin to see and experience prayer in a whole new light. What we need, of course, is a relationship with God—the kind of relationship that enables us simply to trust in the fact that God's grace is sufficient, regardless of whether we experience hardship or happiness.

I realize, of course, that such a perspective is not easily arrived at. The ability to place our lives truly in God's hands and to trust that "all will be well" is something that tends to elude many of us, but this sense of acceptance is, I believe, the intended goal of prayer. While unanswered prayer may prove to be disappointing, it may also prove to be a necessary building block in enabling us to construct the kind of relationship with God that is not dependent upon getting the answers that we want, but upon the answer that we need— the answer that is found in a relationship with God.

While this answered prayer metaphor worked well for Bill King, I believe that we can do better. Ironic as it may be, it is often in our unanswered prayers that we receive the real answer that we are looking for."

Thank you, Brian, and especially thank you, Ron!

Fortnight for Freedom

Bulletin Letter — June 17, 2012

The U.S. Bishops have recently called for what they describe as a "Fortnight for Freedom." The idea is a fourteen day period (June 21-July 4) of prayer, education and action to insist strongly on religious freedom—our first, most cherished liberty, in our nation—and to oppose any possible threat against it. The fourteen days begin on the vigil of the feast that honors John Fischer and Thomas More, martyrs for religious freedom under Henry VIII, and conclude with our Nation's 4th of July Celebration of Independence.

The background behind the "Fortnight for Freedom" is the bishops' concern that recent state and federal laws and proposals appear to violate the conscience rights of some health care providers, as well as religious institutions like Catholic schools, hospitals and social service agencies. They attempt to define "religious" as limited to only service by religious denominations to fellow members and do not view ministry to non-members as "religious at all." As our own bishop has recently stated, this is not a "political struggle," but recognition of the state intruding into the affairs of the Church and even defining what it considers as ministry. The focus here is the Administration's recent healthcare proposal, which attempts to mandate the provision of contraception, sterilization and abortion-inducing drugs.

As the communications director for the Archdiocese of San Francisco recently wrote: "Hidden away in the multitude of regulations accompanying the mandate was a *new definition* of what was to be considered 'religious activity.' This new definition limited 'religious activity' to houses of worship and its congregants. An exemption, therefore, would be given only to a religious entity that serves and teaches its own faithful.

Serving others not of our faith, as do our social services, health care and education, does not qualify as a 'religious activity.' In essence, this new definition redefines what it is to be Catholic."

Frankly, some are concerned that despite the religious rhetoric, "Fortnight for Freedom" may come across as an anti-Obama campaign in an election year. While forty-three Catholic institutions have filed lawsuits in court, others fear that a loss could well establish a very different legal precedent and sharply erode the broad definition of religion presently enjoyed in most current federal laws. Still others object to the intemperate language and hostile rhetoric of at least some of the bishops. One has compared Obama to Stalin and Hitler, while another has said, "The White House is strangling the Catholic Church."

My own take is that prayers for our nation and its religious liberty and the willingness to politely agree to disagree are always in season. The "Fortnight for Freedom" prayer is listed in the foldout. When it comes to politics and voting, the main steps are to get the facts and vote our own conscience. I reprint a slightly more extensive summary, which I have shared with you many times.

"As I've outlined before in this bulletin, in homilies and in adult education, I recommend five steps in our 'political/religious' thinking: 1) to ground ourselves again and again in the values and wisdom of the gospel; 2) to get the actual facts as best we can; 3) to insist that our bishops and spiritual leaders speak out on crucial public issues; 4) to study carefully and prayerfully not just their position but their arguments; 5) to vote our conscience and, if we differ, to remain open to further discussion and revision in the light of Church teaching and leadership.

"A slightly tougher but more practical question comes with public or political advocacy at the local level, like diocese or parish. Here at Christ the King, for the past six years, parishioners have invited support for and against government action on issues that were studied by our Social Justice Committee and viewed as of crucial impact and either in fairly clear harmony or disharmony with Catholic Social teaching. Examples include: discontinuing aid to families with dependent children, food stamps for legal immigrants, hospice for AIDS victims, closure of the School of the Americas, emergency shelter and transitional housing for working families, and petitions to abolish the death penalty.

"Three footnotes need to be added. 1) Our Social Justice Task force needs to do its homework as thoroughly, objectively and conscientiously as possible; 2) their recommendations are only that, an invitation for those who agree to petition, vote or inform themselves further; 3) partisan positions, partisan comments and support or opposition to specific candidates are never appropriate."

Prayer for Religious Liberty

Almighty God, Father of all nations,
For freedom you have set us free in Christ Jesus (Gal 5:1).
We praise and bless you for the gift of religious liberty,
the foundation of human rights, justice, and the common
good. Grant to our leaders the wisdom to protect and promote
our liberties; By your grace may we have the courage to
defend them, for ourselves and for all those who live in this
blessed land. We ask this through the intercession of Mary
Immaculate, our Patroness, and in the name of your Son, our
Lord Jesus Christ, in the unity of the Holy Spirit, with whom
you live and reign, one God, for ever and ever. Amen.

Why Go to Mass? – Part I

Bulletin Letter — January 25, 2004

Recent statistics show a significant decline in the percentage of Catholics attending Mass in the U.S., as well as the frequency with which they do so. Beginning this weekend and following, I want to share a few reflections on "Why Go to Mass." This first reflection is taken largely from a column in *America Magazine* by Fr. James Martin, S.J.

"The past few years have been painful ones for Catholics, especially in this country. If you are divorced and remarried, you may feel unwelcome in your parish. If you are a woman, you may feel anger over the Vatican's stance on ordination. If you are married, you may find yourself at odds with the church's teaching on contraception.

"But it is not just 'liberal' Catholics who struggle. You may feel that the beauty of the Mass has been watered down, and that the mystery that you treasured has been taken away. You may think that too often the 'spirit of Vatican II' is taken to mean that anything goes. You may lament that so many Catholics seem to disregard church teaching and tradition without bothering to learn or understand it. You may have been angered by the hierarchy's increasingly strong opposition to capital punishment, or by the Vatican's opposition to the war in Iraq and its support of the United Nations.

"Finally, no matter what your theological bent, you may feel angered, confused, saddened or disgusted over the sexual abuse scandal.

"In his best-selling book *The Holy Longing*, Ronald Rolheiser, O.M.I., offers nine reasons why one should go to church. They are: 1. Because it is not good to be alone; 2. To take my place within the family of humanity; 3. Because God calls me there; 4. To dispel my fantasies about myself; 5. Because the saints have told me so; 6. To help others with their pathologies and to let them help me with mine; 7. To dream with others; 8. To practice for heaven; and, 9. For the pure joy of it.

"In these times, I think, it is particularly important to focus on the third reason—because God calls me there.

"The church in this country needs help. It needs single and married Catholics, and it needs divorced and remarried Catholics. It needs Catholics who protest at the former School of the Americas, and it needs Catholics who pray at Medjugorge. It needs Call to Action and it needs Opus Dei. It needs conservatives and liberals, men and women, gays and straights.

"As St. Paul wrote, the body of Christ 'does not consist of one member, but of many.' And in order to be healthy the church needs all of its members – especially those who feel in any way marginalized. 'The eye cannot say to the hand, 'I have no need of you.'

"How do we know this? Because in baptism all of us were called by God to be active members of the body of Christ. So while it may be difficult at times to believe that the church wants you, never stop believing that church needs you."

Why Go to Mass? – Part II

Bulletin Letter — February 1, 2004

First the bad news. One of the most familiar complaints heard by priests from parents is, "My kids don't go to Church anymore!"

- One of the most common complaints from irregular churchgoers is, "It's boring," and "I don't get anything out of it."
- Competition for weekend time has become fierce: so many things to see and do; so little time for relaxation, leisure or family. Once upon a time, Sunday church service was the major thing and often the only thing to do on Sunday morning.
- Catholics have been faithful, serious, and regular about Sunday Mass when a persecuted minority and the price for Mass attendance ranged from ridicule (once in America) to imprisonment (early Christians, Iron Curtain). Without second class citizenship and opposition we tend to stop acting like Catholics!
- Since 2003, Protestants have clearly overtaken Catholics in church attendance, for the first time in Gallup polling history. Weekly Church attendance in 1955: Catholics 74%, Protestants 42%; 1969: Catholics 63%, Protestants 37%; 1979: Catholics 52%; Protestants 36%; November 2003: Catholics 45%, Protestants 48%.

A Parishioner's "Sunday Morning Thoughts" (or maybe Saturday evening at 4:45 p.m.): "Another Sunday morning and I sure would like to sleep in . . . . Lots of my friends avoid going to Church; they tell me it's boring and often irrelevant (at least it was when they last attended many years ago!) . . . . They say they have a hard time understanding all that religious stuff that goes on (personally, I find using the computer and following football plays on T.V. are also hard to understand unless I make an effort) . . . . They say a lot hypocrites go to Church (Bishop Ken Untener says criticizing Church because hypocrites show up is like criticizing Weight Watchers because they let fat people in!)

"Why Do I Keep Going? Sometimes I feel the same arguments my friends have: I don't always understand everything that goes on; I don't always like all the people there; the leaders don't do it my way in terms of music, length, topics or language. But I do keeping going and I will keep going."

Next week, the Reasons Why!

Guilt, fear, and family pressure just aren't what they used to be!

Why Go to Mass? – Part III

Bulletin Letter — February 8, 2004

Entirely by coincidence last weekend, Fr. Dibble included in his homily the results of his "survey" on why people go to Mass and came up with seven responses. The ones I liked most were: "I feel better" (that's positive and personal); "I owe God at least one hour a week" (do the math and it's about giving thanks).

Now here are some of my own favorites:

... "My spiritual journey and my life can't be walked alone."

... "A regular celebration with a community of faith nourishes me, and I actually support and contribute something to the life and faith of others, even those I don't know personally."

... "I need to hear the Word and be led and challenged by others, instead of a constant diet of my own choices for reflection, opinion, and prayer (or non-prayer!)."

... "God may be everywhere, but the presence of the living Christ is unique, powerful and, at least at times, almost tangible at Mass—first in our gathering together, then in the Word of Scripture and most of all in Communion."

... "It's about my identity as a Catholic and Christian: regular participation in the Eucharist establishes that identity; regular absence dilutes and threatens that identity."

... "It's the family get-together and meal, and it's my family!"

... "I need to be regularly reminded of who I am before God; and even if I feel 'Lord, I'm not worthy,' we celebrate that I am accepted and loved by God."

... "I need to hear how believers of the past struggled and lived out their faith long before I came on the spiritual scene; at Mass, I feel connected with them and with my loved ones who have passed on."

. . . "It's so nice to feel how other believers want me there and need me there."

. . . "I need help with prayer and I need a community of faith, whether I am at my worst, really on a roll, or just plodding along."

. . . "I go because I want to say, 'Thanks to God, for yet another day and another chance to live, work and grow.'"

An overheard conversation:

"I used to be Catholic." So I asked, "What has taken its place?" He thought a moment and said, "Well, nothing." I asked, "Are you sure? One theory says there's no such thing as an atheist. We always make something or someone into our god." He countered (a little too quickly, I thought), "I'm not an atheist, I'm just not religious," and then he added the ever-familiar platitude and exact quote from Monica Lewinsky to Barbara Walters, "I'm not religious. I'm more, like, spiritual." (Give me strength.) I said, "Oh, I'm sure you're spiritual, but what takes the place of your religion? I mean, like, what do you do Sunday mornings? Who do you pray to? What do you use as a guide for big decisions? What gives direction, meaning and purpose to your life?" His answer was direct, "Gee, I've never thought about those questions before."

To Live or Let Die

From Bulletin — February 4, 2007

In late December Piergiorgio Welby, an Italian poet and quadriplegic suffering from muscular dystrophy, was granted his explicit request when a doctor turned off the ventilator that had been keeping him alive. The Diocese of Rome proceeded to deny him a Christian burial. In my humble, but fairly well informed opinion, that was a serious violation of pastoral care and ministry and a clear contradiction of traditional and official Catholic teaching that there is no obligation to use extraordinary or disproportionate means to prolong life.

Welby had penned an eloquent letter to the President of Italy pleading to be allowed to die. "I love life, Mr. President," he wrote. But after 40 years of battling muscular dystrophy and nine years attached to a ventilator and now losing the capacity to speak or to eat, he wrote, "What is left to me is no longer a life. It is an unbearable torture." He then asked to have the ventilator removed. That request, honored on a regular basis in hospitals across the world, was denied. It caused an uproar in Italy, was denounced as a demand for suicide, and was refused by the Italian courts. After a doctor turned the ventilator off, Welby said, "Thank you," three times to his wife and his friends, and his doctor. Forty-five minutes later he was dead. At least one legislator called for the physician to be charged with homicide and Cardinal Ruini of Rome forbade a Catholic funeral. Later Cardinal Martini, former Archbishop of Milan and once leading papal candidate, criticized the decision, claiming that because of new technology much greater wisdom is needed in order "not to prolong life when it is no longer to a person's benefit."

In its 1980 *Declaration on Euthanasia,* The Vatican officially states, "One cannot impose on anyone the obligation to have recourse to a technique which is already in use but which carries a risk or is burdensome. Such a refusal is not the equivalent of suicide; on the contrary it should be considered as an acceptance of the human condition, or a wish to avoid the application of a medical procedure disproportionate to the results that can be accepted."

Back in 1950, Fr. Gerald Kelly, the foremost moral theologian in the U.S. taught that "no remedy is obligatory unless it offers a reasonable hope of checking or curing a disease . . . no one is obligated to use any means—natural or artificial—if it does not offer a reasonable hope of success in overcoming the patient's condition."

The fact that Welby had also been a public advocate of euthanasia should in no way change Church teaching or pastoral practice on the subject. The request and action taken was precisely the kind of decision that has been explicitly allowed by Catholic moral theologians since at least 1587!

At the end of his long journey towards death, Pope John Paul II declined the option of returning to the hospital where a respirator had assisted his failing breathing and nutrition was supplied through a tube. He said, "Let me go to the house of the Father." No one confused the Pope's action with suicide, nor should they, with Welby's refusal to endure what he described as "the unbearable torture" of being attached to a respirator. Fortunately the Pope was not refused Christian burial too!!

Easter Letter

Bulletin Letter — April 8, 2007

Happy Easter and welcome to all friends, family, visitors as well as long time parishioners! Easter is a time and season that brings together in our roomy Church people of many diverse levels of faith and belief to celebrate Jesus and draw closer to one another and to our God.

Author James Joyce once described the Catholic Church as "here comes everybody!" Recently, when Fr. Daniel Berrigan had a book dedicated to himself as a "Christian," he corrected the author to say he had left out one phrase: "would-be." We are all "would-be Christians." Easter brings together both "seekers" and "finders" (or at least those who think they have found it all). It gathers once-a-year-Catholics and daily Mass communicants. It welcomes the rigorist and the unsure, the liberal and the conservative, the convinced Catholic, curious non-believers, and everyone in between.

There's an important, life-giving lesson here. We cannot build a society or a church with just liberals or just conservatives. To build true community we need to work with more than just those who are like-minded. A community, church or parish built with just the like-minded is hardly worth belonging to, because it reflects neither what's best inside the human spirit nor, for those of us who are Christians, the inclusive embrace of Christ.

There are those who believe that life and the difficult problems of our nations, our planet and its people are all a matter of fate, or maybe karma or even reincarnation. Easter says and celebrates the exact opposite. Now, the exact opposite of fate is not chance or random happenings, or to grimly say just about anything can happen. The opposite of fate is really hope. It is to say, as we do in Jesus' death and resurrection, or in God's amazing love, that everything is possible. One author has said that hope is "the adrenaline of the soul"; it gives us the energy, the vision and the strength to go forward and to work at and do noble things with our life and our world.

We live our personal lives in a world deeply in need of hope and noble actions. May we be a community that hopes together and works together for greater peace, for honest politics, for just and caring societies, for an end to violence and terror, for a welcome to the homeless and the immigrant, for the safety and quick return of our young people at war. In other words, may we be an Easter people who live out a rugged, realistic and practical Easter hope.

Easter Sunday

Bulletin Letter — March 31, 2013

A Happy and Joy-filled Easter to you all and a special welcome to those visiting us for the celebration: families reunited, students home from school, neighbors dropping in. Welcome, all. As James Joyce famously described the Catholic Church "here comes everybody!"

While we celebrate Easter as a family and faith community, it's amazing how many different understandings and beliefs there are about Easter and Resurrection. I think many of us differ in our understanding of what Easter meant for Jesus, what it means for our loved ones, and what it means for ourselves.

Some people have the limited and mistaken notion that Easter faith means to remember that Jesus once left behind an empty tomb and walked around as a resuscitated cadaver rather than remaining a lifeless corpse. Rather, Easter faith means something more radical for Jesus, for our loved ones, and for us.

For Jesus. Scripture makes it clear this was no way near being a case of successful CPR. This was an entirely different experience of life, but to his closest acquaintances both awesome and frightening, reassuring and real. Everything was changed and our best description is of a risen, living Christ of the Universe, not just a surprisingly healthy Jesus of Nazareth.

For our loved ones. We believe that nothing in the universe is ever lost, and somehow it is all about relationships. At the heart or end of our life is consciousness and relationships. We believe that in the life giving Spirit of Christ Jesus, both remain; nothing is lost; our loved ones live on.

For ourselves. Our Easter faith is that "resurrection" or "eternal life" do not just refer to something way at the end of life or "at the end of the line." It is also the texture and the quality of how we live right now. "Resurrection" points to the real possibility and power of a life of hope, rather than despair, a life of loving compassion and service, rather than resentment and indifference. That is the kind of life our parish community seeks to live in good years and in bad. In this past year alone we have retired one Pope, received a new one, and certainly for a while were Popeless but not hopeless. This Easter we *remember*, we *celebrate* and we *believe* what Christ Jesus announced long ago and makes possible today, "I have come that you might have life and have it to the full" (John 10:10).

As a parish community, our simple, straightforward mission statement and identity is, "To Hear the Gospel and Make a Difference." Our parish community is remarkable and generous in working at that. Among the many ways we try to hear the Gospel, we always include adult learning and adult education. When it comes to making a difference, two outstanding examples have got to be, in these recent economic hard times, our Job Network Ministry and our St. Vincent de Paul volunteers.

Our Job Network Ministry over the last three years has served almost 500 people. Currently there are 130 job seekers being helped. The help comes in the form of job-skills training and networking, small group meetings to share ideas, leads and contacts, connection to immediate job leads, and regular spiritually based messages. We know that more than 100 people have found jobs due to the supportive environment and at least one suicide was adverted.

A second way our community makes a difference is through our St. Vincent de Paul Society and its volunteer members. Every day of the week, Monday through Friday, they meet and help the needy who come to our front door. Thousands of families and individuals are aided because of your generosity. Today a second collection is taken up at all Masses for their important work. Thank you for your support!

The Pope's Social Encyclical

Bulletin Letter — July 26, 2009

The Pope didn't just break his wrist! He also broke his image. This July he issued his third and long-awaited social encyclical, a personal papal letter on the social teaching of the Church and its application today. It will stand well in the series of such documents dating back to Leo XIII's "*Rerum Novarum*" (*Of New Things*). That1891 document is the foundation stone of the Catholic social teaching tradition—a tradition that broke ground away from "thou shalt not lie." "thou shalt not kill," and "thou shalt not steal," to address the condition of labor and the need for everything from child labor laws, minimum and living wages, the right to organize (horror of horrors—unions!), and the right to collective bargaining. As one commentator writes, "Benedict XVI has made a habit of refuting his own stereotype. None of his three encyclicals, least of all this one, confirms the image of "Ratzinger, the conservative autocrat."

No, I don't expect many of you to run out and buy a copy of "*Caritas in Veritate.*" I also don't expect this closely reasoned and thickly written document to make anyone's bestseller list. Still, it is an important landmark in the social justice teaching of the Church. It is one that will be hotly debated for years to come. One American neo-conservative has already written it off as a "duck-billed platypus!" consisting of agreeable (to him) lines that the Pope must have written mixed with "justice and peace" lines that someone else must have inserted! This is reminiscent of William F. Buckley dismissing the great social encyclical, "*Mater et Magistra*," by Pope John XXIII in the 1960s with the snide remark, "*Mater* (mother), *Si: Magistra* (teacher), *No!*"

If I had to summarize the ground-breaking work in Pope Benedict's letter, it would be with three really deep and profound phrases: "integral human development," "gift," and "fraternity."

Integral Human Development—Ever since Vatican II (1962-1965) and the writings of Pope Paul VI (1963-1978), the scope of evangelization (which all accept as the Church's job), has been pushed to bring social justice within the agenda of the Church's main business. However, "Preaching the Gospel" and "working for social justice" still seem to be separate. The Pope now brings the two halves emphatically together to make one whole. "The Whole Church, in all her being and acting—when she proclaims, when she celebrates, when she performs acts of charities is engaged in promoting integral human development . . . . Authentic human development concerns the whole person in every dimension." There simply is no spiritual pathway that bypasses integral human development, which leads to Christ and finds its measurement and criteria in Christ. This central idea, the fusion of spirituality and social action under the banner of integral human development enables Benedict to turn to contemporary crises: the current financial crisis, the crisis of globalization and migration, and the impact of each on integral human development.

Gift and Fraternity—Discussing modern finance, Benedict draws a line between a "capitalist economy" aimed at maximum profit and a "civil market economy" aimed at the common good. It includes the concept of "gift," which is not oriented solely by profit, and he encourages "fraternity," a generalized sort of friendship between equals that respects diversity. A civil market promotes something for which people already possess an instinct; they need and want to be able to "give."

Pope Benedict also places his hopes in the United Nations. "There is an urgent need of a true world political authority to bring about integral and timely disarmament, food security, and peace, to guarantee the protection of the environment and to regulate migration."

The Pope already has a reputation for being "green," and he puts his whole rhetorical weight behind it. He calls for a reform of lifestyles and the reeducation of conscious choices as part of "a covenant between human beings and the environment." This too is the Church's business for the sake of integral human development.

As one editor has put it, "This remarkable and intelligent man, now in his eighties, seems to have regained the originality of mind that once made him one of the most innovative voices at Vatican II. Half-a-century later, he still has new things to say, well worth hearing, well worth waiting for. And no stereotype could ever begin to describe him."

Why Do I Stay?

Bulletin Letter — August 2, 2009

Next week, we get to meet and welcome our new bishop, Salvatore Cordileone, on two different occasions. On Monday morning, he will be here for a diocesan-wide meeting of Catholic School principals and pastors, including an 11:30 a.m. Mass which he will celebrate with us. Then on next Sunday at 12:15 p.m., he will be with us for Mass and followed by a reception as we bless (and show off!) our newly redone church. I look forward to his coming and the church blessing; however at quite another level I feel like we almost need a caution label reading: "Warning! This week may be harmful to your spiritual health!"

The reason I say that is, however delighted we may be with the bishop himself and with our newly redone church, being Church, being Catholic, and our spiritual life is not about hierarchy or bishop, and most certainly not about church buildings. Whether we celebrate in a tent or parish gym, in parish hall or out on the lawn, with or without any building at all, being Church means being a people (with Pope and bishops included) who encounter Christ, celebrate gospel and Eucharist, and witness through caring and justice.

The question I've run into repeatedly this summer from kind and thoughtful Catholics and grumpy, unhappy ones as well is, "Why do I stay?" Some of you may disagree with me, but I have never met anyone who stays in the Church because of a bishop (although some have left because of bishops or pastors, but that's quite a different issue). And although we all have our favorite and least favorite churches and our different preferences when it comes to design and architecture, I don't know anyone who stays or leaves the Church because of a given church building.

This summer, I've heard two different sets of reasons for "why I stay" which I find both interesting and helpful. The first I've already shared with you in two outdoor homilies, which I repeat here from James Carroll's recent best seller, *Practicing Catholic*.

He writes: "We maintain our loyalty to the Church because we cannot live without it. The Church gives us a language with which to speak of God, it gives us a meaning that is God. The Church feeds us with the Eucharist, keeps the story of Jesus alive in the preaching of the Word, marks our journey through life with the Sacraments, and underwrites our participation in the community that transcends time and space."

The second and more intriguing answer comes from Benedictine Sister, author, feminist and renowned spiritual guide Joan Chittister, who was recently asked in a question-and-answer forum, "Why don't you leave the Church?" Given the setting, she listed her reasons as: first, the Catholic Church is the greatest treasury of spiritual traditions we have; secondly, the Catholic Church is the only real depository of great women through the ages that exists; thirdly, whatever our disappointments or complaints, the Church always has the capacity for self-conversion (delayed though it may be); and finally, "It's my family."

You may or may not agree with these two sets of answers, but the real question is more personal than that: Why do *you* stay? And what does your staying demand of you?

Pentecost & The Holy Spirit

Bulletin Letter — May 23, 2010

Happy Pentecost!! Hope you remembered to wear red today. If you did, thank you for decorating our church and ourselves; if you forgot, don't worry, the Spirit and today's gospel are all about forgiveness!

The Holy Spirit is always at work prodding, renewing and reforming our Church as the People of God. Sometimes it's through anointed leadership, like Councils (try Vatican II for example); sometimes it's through heroic figures like our martyrs and saints, and unexpected surprising figures like Pope John XXIII and Oscar Romero; sometimes it's by tragic, embarrassing and downright evil events. I believe the current clergy sex abuse scandal is one such event. Even out of tragedy and wrongdoing the Spirit renews the Church and hopefully challenges us to be more transparent, accountable and humble. With the very important Safe Environment Training evening coming up, it's an appropriate time, not only to urge some of you to be there, but to count the ways that some good has come out of such abuse and also to mention where, I think, we still fall short.

Here in the U.S. at least, bishops have agreed to a "zero tolerance" policy when it comes to clergy abuse. A charter for the protection of children and young people has been put in place. Each diocese is to be audited annually for compliance, with on-site visits every three years (this October for us). Each diocese is asked to have a review board made up primarily of professional lay people (ours was among the first). Under the leadership of Sr. Barbara Flannery, the Diocese of Oakland established the nation's first outreach program for survivors of clergy abuse. Victims' assistance programs have been put in place. Background checks (through Megan's Law) are now required of all parish volunteers. Fingerprinting checks are in place for all clergy and staff, with a goal of eventually covering all parish volunteers (this year, we plan to reach all in Youth Ministry, R.E. catechists, CYO coaches, and overnight chaperones). All our children, both in our parish school and R.E. program, participate in a "Shield the Vulnerable" curriculum. Safe Environment training is now in place and required of most parish volunteers . . . . Heads up, everyone, a one-hour training will take place this Thursday evening in Church!!

Where I believe we have fallen short is that no U.S. Bishop has stepped down or offered to resign admitting in some way responsibility for what has taken place, knowingly or unknowingly, on his watch.

As the scandal of clergy abuse and episcopal mishandling surfaces in Ireland and around Europe, it's heartening to hear Pope Benedict XVI distancing himself from those who criticize the media as the problem, rather than as the beginning of a solution. He has recognized the importance of forgiveness and compassion, but insisted that justice come first—"Forgiveness cannot substitute for justice." He also states that the Church is not so much being persecuted or unfairly criticized, but rather the problem "is born from sins within the Church"!

Could the Holy Spirit be hard at work? As the Church's Magisterium and Vatican II teach, "The Church must always be reforming itself!"

The Second Vatican Council (IV)

Bulletin Letter — December 1, 2013

One of the greatest gifts in my lifetime has been the work of the Second Vatican Council. This Wednesday, December 4th, we celebrate the fiftieth anniversary of its greatest achievement. In a landslide vote of 2,147 bishops in favor and four against, the Council set in motion a reshaping of the way Roman Catholics worship, unlike anything tried before. You may not all remember it, but until 1963 Catholic worship, especially the Sunday Mass, was fixed, rubrical, clergy-oriented, unchanging, and often unintelligible. Our worship was largely stressing external actions and what the priest did with his back to the people "up there," while the people were passive viewers. And it was all in Latin! Fifty years ago this week, the bishops at Vatican II changed all this. Before long, laymen and laywomen read the Scripture for the first time and became Eucharistic Ministers. Catholics received the consecrated bread in their hands and were offered consecrated wine from the cup and a wide variety of Scripture readings were introduced. Four principles guided the bishops' renewal in worship:

1. Full active participation by everyone as our right and duty;
2. Adaption of worship to local circumstances, especially important in missionary countries;
3. Authority of local Bishops and Bishops' Conferences to make decisions for local circumstances and culture;
4. Bringing worship in line with contemporary special needs, education and maturity of Catholics.

As you may have noticed, some of these principles are being challenged, compromised, and even reversed today. A dramatic recent example must be the new English translation of the Mass for English speaking countries, imposed on us all since 2011.

To celebrate this important work and look at the future we have invited a delightful and outstanding speaker to join us this Friday night. Together with Fr. David Pettingill, we will look at the way we have worshipped and the way we will worship in the future. This is an evening not to be missed.

Welcome, Fr. Dave! Don't miss him!

Advent is also celebrated as a season of women, especially of Mary, as we wait for the birth of her newborn child. During the four weekends of Advent our homily time will be shared by four women parishioners, once again in recognition

of their giftedness and giving. This week's homilist is
Marcy Fox, Ed.D., a member of Christ the King parish for

Welcome, Marcy!

twenty-seven years. She has been a teacher and administrator in the field of Religious Studies in Catholic high schools for over 30 years. She is also an adjunct professor in the School of Education at the University of San Francisco. She currently teaches full-time at Carondelet High School in Concord.

It has been three years since our last Priest Convocation! Bishop Barber has asked all parish priests to join him for this year's Convocation in Napa. We'll begin this Monday afternoon and continue until Thursday. Fr. Timoney, Fr. Cotter, and I plan to be there. It will give us all a chance to look at where our diocese has been and where it is going next. Be sure to assist us with your prayers.

A Thanksgiving Prayer

O God, when I have food,
help me to remember the hungry;
When I have work,
help me to remember the jobless;
When I have a home,
help me to remember those
who have no home at all;
When I am without pain,
help me to remember those who suffer …
And remembering,
help me to destroy my complacency,
bestir my compassion,
and be concerned enough to help
by word and deed,
those who cry out
for what we take for granted.
Amen.

By Samuel F. Pugh

UNCENSORED . . .

The final grouping is entitled *Uncensored* and predictably it goes a little longer than the bulletin issues and four-minute specials. Mostly, it is comprised of homilies, everything by myself or others whom I consider significant. The first includes homilies given by the late Fr. Declan Dean, including his question, "What would Jesus do today?" and his final homily given on the weekend before his death in December, 2010. Three other significant homilies would have to include Kate Doherty, our young and extremely articulate Associate Pastor, a homily given by Fr. Dan Danielson recently at our 52nd class reunion, and the homily given by Bishop John Cummins at my Retirement Mass. Finally, there are several of my homilies which, for one reason or another, I consider uncensored or at least significant.

If Jesus Returned

Homily of February 14, 2012
Based on Mark 8:14-21
by Father Declan Deane

So that little lecture by Jesus has been called a series of bombshells. Another writer, G.K. Chesterton, a great English Catholic writer, said that to understand a passage like that you should learn to stand on your head, because Jesus sets the world's values upside down. And, you know at that time people did not respond very well to Him. There might have been a huge crowd at one time but, one by one, they all faded away and finally there was only a tiny little nucleus left, because they were alienated by the things He said and did. And some of them turned completely against Him.

So I asked myself the question, "What would happen if Jesus came back today, February, 2010?" What if He did the things and said the kind of things that He did 2000 years ago? Would I follow Him? Would you? Would many people? How would we respond? So, I allowed my imagination to run a little bit riot, and it went something like this.

Jesus landed at SFO. He was invited to address the Commonwealth Club. The scheduled lecturer was postponed until next year; it was meant to be given by Deepak Chopra, entitled "Finding Peace of Mind." The first thing Jesus did was ask how much the fee was to be and they told him $50,000. He said, "Please go out into the street and distribute it among the beggars and the homeless people."

Then in His lecture He said, "If you want to find peace of mind, avoid greed in all its forms. The best thing you can do to obtain peace of mind is to sell what you have—your homes, your cars, your property. Give everything you have to the poor, and then you will truly find peace of mind." At the end of the lecture people came out shaking their heads a little bit in bafflement and saying, "What a strange man. He didn't have a whole lot of comfort to offer us. Perhaps we should have stuck with Deepak Chopra." The archbishop of San Francisco invited Jesus to dinner with all the religious leaders of the city. Jesus said He would be happy to go to the dinner the next evening, but that this evening He had a prior commitment. He planned to dine at a restaurant in the Castro with friends from the gay and lesbian, bisexual and transgender community. He invited the religious leaders to join Him, but they politely declined.

From then on, Jesus was picketed wherever He went by members of the Christian Coalition. They carried banners saying, "This cannot be the Messiah. He welcomes sinners and dines with them." Jesus visited San Quentin prison, and He called a press conference and stated, "All human life is sacred, from the unborn child in the womb to my humble friends on death row. Each one of them has an angel that worships day and night before My Father in heaven."

By the things He said and did, Jesus alienated both liberals and conservatives. Day by day, the numbers of His followers decreased. But among those followers were some faithful women who seldom left Jesus' side. Their presence was a great boon to the hoard of paparazzi who trailed Jesus everywhere. The Papal Nuncio approached Jesus and tactfully suggested that He might invite the women to go home. "They are giving a bad impression," he said. "People are beginning to say that women can play as important a part in Your community as men." To which Jesus replied, "Have you not read what my servant Paul wrote, 'In Christ there is neither male nor female, but all are one in Him?'"

Later that week, it was announced that Jesus was being investigated by the Sacred Congregation for the Doctrine of the Faith. As He walked along the street there were always crowds surrounding him. One day, a man who was identified as a leading member of the Mafia, in fact he was commonly referred to as the godfather, was very eager to see Jesus. Being short of stature, he climbed up into a tree. Jesus walked past, looked up, saw him and said, "Come down, godfather. I plan to dine at your house today." Delightedly, the godfather invited all his friends to his mansion. FBI agents went up and down, faithfully recording the license plates. At the end of the meal the godfather rose and said, "Ladies and gentlemen, I have an announcement to make. Here and now I have decided to give half of everything that I own to the poor, and if I have defrauded anyone—and regrettably I have—I am going to repay them fourfold." Jesus smiled and said, "Salvation has come to this house, because you too are a child of God." Next day the *San Francisco Chronicle* carried a banner headline that said, "Jesus Loves Crime Baron." Many politicians now jumped on the opportunity to denounce Jesus as a dangerous radical. Everywhere He went, He was shadowed by weary local and federal agents.

Finally, one day He was accosted by a Muslim, a wealthy man, who had a sick servant. "Sir," he said, "I am not a Christian myself, but I can tell that you are from God. Now, I am not worthy that You should enter under my roof. Say but the word and my servant will be healed." Jesus said to him, "Your servant is healed as of this very moment." And then He turned to the crowd and said, "This man has more faith than all the Christians I have met." This was the crowning blow for many people. Jesus was warned that His life was in danger, and He was forced to flee to another place.

So that's how I allowed my imagination to roam free. Maybe it'd be a little bit like that if Jesus returned. Certainly, it's imaginable that He would have done and said much the same things as He did when He was here 2000 years ago.

The question then arises, how would you and I respond? Would we give Him praise and blessing and honor, or would we, like the majority of people, either drift away or turn against Him?

Let's take a few moments of silence to ask ourselves the question, "How would we respond to someone so wonderfully disconcerting as Jesus of Nazareth?"

Procrastination

Homily of December 5, 2010
Based on Matthew 3:1-12
by Father Declan Deane

Sometimes, when I've told the same story twice in a homily,
I think there might be two accounts for it, so I give myself
absolution. The first account could be: well, I've been out of
commission for a while, and maybe they don't remember that
I've told this story. The second one would be: I'm getting up
there in years, and maybe I don't remember I gave this story.

But this story took place in Ireland, it really did, so you
know it's truthful.

A friend of mine called John was clearing out his attic, and
he found an old ticket for shoe repairs, only it was dated 1955.
Out of curiosity, he got in his car and drove down to Dublin
(not this Dublin, the *big* Dublin) and sure enough there was
a shop that said "shoe repairs," and he rang the bell. After a
while, a man opens the door. He is a crotchety kind of an old
man, and he says, "What do you want?" John handed him the
ticket, and the man peered shortsightedly at it and said, "That
will take a while." So, he disappeared into the back of the shop
and was gone a very long time. Eventually, John could hear him
traipsing back in and in an even more quiet, tempered mood he
looked at John, handed him the ticket and said, "Those shoes
will be ready on Wednesday."

Now, that's called procrastination. John the Baptist was
not a procrastinator. He said, "The Kingdom of God is at hand.
Whatever you need to do that's good and right, do it now, for
the Kingdom of God is at hand." I've tried to do that all my life,
but I've never really managed it. I always seem to put things off
for a day or a week or a month or a year or 50 years.

A priest friend of mine in Ireland took me in hand one time. He said, "I think I have the solution for you, because I had the same problem and I cured myself."

I said, "How did you manage that?"

And he said, "Oh, someone gave me this book called *Overcoming Procrastination*. I read it and now I don't procrastinate anymore." So, he lent me the book, and he met me about six months later and said, "Well, did the book help?"

And I said, "Well, Brendan, I haven't quite got around to reading it yet."

John the Baptist would say to us, "Don't be like that. If there is something you need to do, do it now because the Kingdom of God is at hand." And he said, "Now is the time to act," and words that were later repeated by St. Paul, "Now is the acceptable time, now is the day of salvation."

So, here are three suggestions, things you might like to try. Attempt any one and you're fine.

One would be: Be reconciled to someone that has something against you. Be reconciled. Before I left Ireland, I had a row with the very man that I liked very much. His name was Andy. He was a Jesuit brother, and he was in charge of the plant, the retreat house, where I was giving retreats, and he was in charge of getting the plant ready for all the retreats. But one time he let me down in a big way! Nothing was ready, everything was a mess. I gave him a piece of my mind, which I hate doing, and afterwards I felt guilty. I really felt I shouldn't have spoken so strongly. So, I went back to Andy and said, "Andy, I'm really sorry. I apologize." And we hugged and that was the end of it. But, you know, he seemed to me the healthiest member of our community. He jogged, he ran in marathons, but one day he ran in a marathon and just dropped dead suddenly and without warning. I often ask myself the question, "What if I hadn't apologized? How would I feel as the years went by?" I think I would feel very, very badly. I'm glad I did it. It was good for him, it was good for me. Don't put it off.

Secondly, would be to tell someone you love that you love them and show it. It's good for you and it's good for them. I come from a culture, the Irish culture, where we're not very good at that. We kind of say, "Well, they know that I love them. I don't have to tell them. It's all implicit." In our family, our mother was like that. She rarely said, "I love you." We knew she did, but I think we would have liked to hear her say it. And you know, toward the end of her life she changed, and one day, at the end of every call and at the end of every visit, she would say, "I love you." It was good for her and it was good for us, and we knew she meant it.

Thirdly, do something completely different, either like as an Advent action or just for the sake of doing something completely different. I made a resolution many years ago, actually 50 years ago, that I would try to learn Spanish. And I kept my resolution 50 years later. I went to Spain, to Mexico, and to Guadalajara (a beautiful city, a beautiful language) and I learned quite a bit of Spanish. I was glad I did. It was something completely daring and completely different.

So this is the message that John the Baptist has for you and me today. "Don't put off any longer . . . ." Listen to the voice of that wonderful saint who pointed to the savior and said, "This is the lamb of God who takes away the sins of the world." And whether you reconciled with someone or whether you tell someone you love them and show it, or whether you do something daring and different, you know that you will be following the example and the advice of St. John the Baptist who said, "Reform your lives, the Kingdom of God is at hand. Now is the time to act; now is the acceptable time; now is the day of salvation."

Prepare the Way

Homily of December 9, 2012
Based on Luke 3:1-6
by Kate Doherty, Associate Pastor

Today's gospel tells of the Old Testament prophets preparing us for the teaching and arrival of Christ, who would change things forever. I have always loved John the Baptist, because he was a wild man living in the desert, speaking the truth. I love him because he actually served as the bridge for me to start believing in the Church.

At 17 years of age, I went from a teenager who felt that the Bible was hypocritical nonsense and that religion was for silly people who couldn't think for themselves, to a 17 year old who was a leader in my youth group and was attending Mass on my own without my parents, because they didn't go. I can honestly say how I went from there to standing here all started with John the Baptist. As a kid I loved adventure stories. I grew up pretending to be Indiana Jones and forcing my younger brother to be my sidekick. My father loved westerns and I grew to love the heroes in those stories as well, such as The Lone Ranger, sick of the triviality of society, leveling their own brand of justice. I guess I still do.

I think that is why John the Baptist was the first biblical character that captured my imagination. He was in the wilderness, ate locusts and honey (my diet is vegan, by the way), dressed in camel hair, and knew something that everybody else just didn't. I can remember feeling thrilled and empowered at the idea, when these insincere religious leaders showed up wanting to be baptized just for show. John sent them away calling them a "brood of vipers." He was brave enough to speak out against the king and queen, which was what led to him being beheaded.

Thinking back on it now, what really sort of resonated with me back then was that this prophet—God's prophet--was calling them and me to live more authentically. Living in a world where I had never known a president you could trust, where satire and bitterness were the marks of intelligence, where irony spoke more truth because politics, religion and youth were more about entertainment and money than truth telling. I was raised to believe that smart means skeptical. So, suddenly to hear a prophet from thousands of years ago acknowledging how sad that is and imploring me to rise above it felt real. It felt like I suddenly saw some truth in Scripture that I had never recognized was there before, and it made me want to take a closer look at everything else and see what else I had been missing.

St. Paul was knocked off his horse on his way to Damascus. My conversion was slightly less dramatic, but in retrospect it did feel theatrical. My high school drama club was performing *Godspell*, and I became intrigued with this figure of John the Baptist. Just about the same time, a leader in my youth group who must have been really fed up with my bad attitude and negativity, decided to write me a letter. It said, "Kate, I don't know how someone who says so many things written in scripture can say that they hate the Bible." What followed were three pages of quotes from me, mirrored by quotes from the Gospel. The one that really stuck with me was the first one on the list which quoted a 17-year-old me saying, "Why do we try so hard to label God—to make God human—or think of God as a 'he' sitting somewhere judging everyone? If there is really a God, it's nothing like that! If there is a God, God would be more like love." Underneath was a quote from John's Gospel, "God is love."

I'll never forget the feeling of awe that washed over me. Something that I felt to be true to my core was right there in Scripture! At 17, I had no idea that the Bible was written by a lot of different people, and I thought the little name on the Gospel was the person who wrote it. So, of course, I immediately equated the Gospel of John with my new idol, John the Baptist. This simple note and the eccentric prophet were enough to make me take pause and listen. It opened me up to the idea that there was something deeper going on in this faith tradition. To be honest, the more I listened, the more I realized I agreed with Jesus and scripture and the Church. This was a complete shock to me—to discover that the more I understood the less I disagreed and that was a pretty rare feeling for me at the time.

As I start this new journey as Associate at Christ the King, I admit I have all the anxieties and reservations that come with any life transition but, I was comforted today when I realized that I was going to start the journey reflecting on the same prophet that started it all for me. John calls for us to mean what we say, to do things with genuine purpose and intent. He wants us to prepare the way. And, when John calls us to prepare the way, he's referring to Christ's way which is the way of love. So, this morning we are all being called to prepare the way of love.

To be honest, I hate preparation. It's the hard part; it's the real work. Here we are in the midst of the holiday season and think about all the stress and agony that comes with the preparation: the cooking, the cleaning, the shopping, trying to make sure everything is just right for the big day. At first, it makes me shudder at the thought of preparing the way of the Lord. Is preparing a Christmas party this much of a nightmare? What does preparing the way of the Lord entail? I don't think I can handle it.

The key here is remembering what kind of party it is you're throwing. Preparing Christ's way means opening your heart and forgiving. It means tapping into joy and making sure that everyone around you has as much, if not more, joy than you. Not that that's an easy task by any means, but it is certainly less scary than hosting the most perfect and holy welcome back party for Jesus.

We all have to think hard about what we have to do in preparing. Some of us have to start loving ourselves a little bit more. Some of us need to acknowledge that our needs and our family's needs are not more important than anyone else's. Openly I think, if we thought a little bit more of preparing the way of love into our holiday preparations, we would all be a little happier. Imagine Jesus is coming to your house for Christmas. Do you want to greet him bleary-eyed with a gorgeous tray of gourmet appetizers, and an immaculate Martha Stewart-level decorated house that is empty, empty because the teen daughter left in tears after you told her that she wasn't bringing her deadbeat boyfriend over to meet the Lord. Your spouse redirected his stress to a bottle of wine and passed out somewhere on a couch. Your son left days ago, unable to bear listening to you and your daughter fight, and let's not even mention your mother who refused to come until that black sheep sister of yours was invited. I think Jesus would take one look around and politely dismiss Himself to your crazy neighbor's house. You know the one I'm talking about—the one with the tacky decorations that you hate every year, always cornering you in the driveway for a chat.

I think Jesus would be perfectly happy to be greeted by a smiling cast of misfits whose food isn't great, who forgot to get the cards out this year, but who are undeniably filled with love. Don't take me wrong. I'm obviously describing the party Jesus excuses himself from, from my own experience. We love each other and that's why we fight, and it's why we try so hard to make everything perfect. That's okay, as long as we take a minute to listen carefully to that lone voice in the wilderness that's reminding us that the real preparation this season is supposed to be about love.

When the Cold North Wind Blows

Homily of August 1, 1999
Based on Matthew 14:13-21

That gospel passage of the loaves and fishes is a very important one in the life of the Church. You can tell, because it is one of the few scenes in the life of Christ that you find in all four Gospels. All four writers said this is important. In fact, Matthew repeats it twice, in two slightly different versions, it's so important. It's very clear that the intent of that story is to point to the Eucharist, where Jesus blesses bread, breaks it, and feeds us with Himself. It's very clear that the lesson from that passage is that Jesus is the bread of life, and Jesus is the bread for our journey and for our daily lives. Another lesson is in the other version from Matthew, it's a little boy that has the loaves and fishes in this huge crowd, and what a difference one person can make.

It also gives you a little feel of the time of the life of Jesus, how revolutionary He was. In a society where they were strictly divided into social castes and classes, where authorities put the poor down and did not want to see them, and where they were not even counting women and children, Jesus gathers them all together, and has them share meals. Can you imagine being an authority in Jerusalem, and hearing there's a guy up in Galilee who's gathering thousands of people, across social barriers, to feed one another, and move on to another meal, after another meal, after another meal, after another meal, until his death and crucifixion. A very important passage, but I don't want to talk to you about that today.

I want to talk to you about the second reading at Mass, which is Paul's lines from his letter to the Romans. Many people call this the most important single piece in the whole scripture. It's Chapter 8 of Romans, verses 35, 37, 38, 39—four lines that are really important, and I think we need to reflect on them.

There's a famous craftsman, who was an artist and a maker of violins. He always taught his pupils and his apprentices, that the best wood for making violins came from the north side of the tree, because the north side of the tree is always seasoned by a cold north wind, again and again. That seasoning gives a special, beautiful sound that no other wood can duplicate. I mention it, because it works that way for people too. So often, it's suffering and tragedy and hard times and difficulties that lead us to produce wondrous works. You see it in music and in the arts. Handel, for example, was worse than being on welfare, poverty stricken, and entirely paralyzed on his right side, when he sat down to compose the Messiah and the Halleluiah chorus.

Beethoven came from a very dysfunctional family, and by the age of 28 he had lost his hearing completely. When he composed and conducted the great 9th Symphony, he could not hear what they were playing. And he could not hear the thunderous applause at the end of his great work.

One of my favorite paintings is of the "Angelus." I don't know how many of you can know of the work, it shows workers in the field pausing to pray the "Angelus." Jean Francois Millet painted it about a 100 years ago. When he started painting, he wrote that day, "We have no fuel (cold winter), and we have no food." And with hands so cold he could hardly hold the brush, he painted that masterpiece. It works for music, and it works for art, and I think it works for life too.

I reflect on this, because I think you might say we've felt something of a cold north wind coming through our parish community for the last five or six months. Our full-time Associate Pastor Margo has found her long battle with leukemia becoming ever more challenging in recent months. And our community has had more than its share of sickness and death in the last few months. We've lost a lot of long-time parishioners, like Frank Isola, Nancy White, Eileen Van Heel, Tom Menesini, and Tony Mora, as well as the loss through suicide of two dear and lovely young people. Then in mid-May, we lost our school through fire.

It sometimes feels like a cold north wind is blowing, and that also seems to be the case in the broader Church. Just two quick examples. A few weeks ago, the Vatican publicly punished a priest and a nun who have been doing very good and necessary work among gay and lesbian Catholics. To many, that seems like a cold north wind. And certainly last week's revelation about Bishop Patrick Zieman of Santa Rosa, and his resignation, has also been a cold north wind.

I want to share with you four things that I find helpful when that cold wind is blowing, whether it's through our church or through our personal lives.

The first thing is, with the Church, it's no surprise. I know that, and it helps me that it's no surprise. Church problems, and problems with Church bureaucracy and with Church people, are not a surprise. I learned a long time ago in history class, and then I learned from personal experience, that we are an imperfect Church made up of saints and sinners at every level, with no exceptions. We are struggling and faltering at the same time. And when these things come, it's no surprise.

The second thing that helps me is to know that the Church is not its particular leaders, not even its personal heroes, of which I have many in the Church, and most of the time they inspire us, and once in a while they fail us. The Church is first of all the community of disciples, those of us trying to follow Jesus. We are the Church. That's why, when people in recent months have come up and offered their sympathy and say how difficult it is, I say, "Not necessary, not so." We are a wonderful, thriving community, a wonderful, thriving parish and church. We have a wonderful staff, highly talented and doing wonderful things. We have wonderful parishioners with gifts and talents. When we look at our lives, the blessings, if we count them, far outnumber and outweigh any cold winds blowing from any direction, and in any number.

The third thing is, there is a sense in which difficulties reveal and bring out the best in us. The school fire was an example when our neighboring congregations stepped up and offered their facilities, and our parishioners stepped up and offered their talents and help. Another example is Father Padraig, where so much support and prayer came for him.

I don't know if you remember, there's a movie with Dustin Hoffman, called *Little Big Man*. Toward the end, there's a touching scene in which an elderly Indian named Old Lodgeskins has lost his physical health and he's gone blind, and he knows he's dying, and he begins to pray to God in these words: "Lord God, I thank you for having made me a human being. I thank you for giving me life and for giving me eyes to see and enjoy your world. But most of all, Lord, I thank you for my sickness and my blindness, because I have learned more from these than from my health and from my sight."

The fourth and most important thing that I find helpful is the conviction that our safety, our security, our certainty, our strength, our hope, comes from our God and nowhere else. It comes from Jesus Christ. That's what Paul is telling us in that second reading, and that's what I've been talking about. "Dear brothers and sisters, what will separate us from the love of Christ: will anguish or distress or persecution, or famine or nakedness or peril or cold north winds? No. In all these things we conquer overwhelmingly through the One who loves us. For I am convinced that neither death nor life, neither things we are going through now, nor future things we may have to go through, neither powers, not height nor depth, nor any creature will be able to separate us from the love of God in Christ Jesus our Lord." And that's the truth. Amen.

Forgiveness: Healthy and Not Destructive

Homily of September 12, 1999

Forgiveness . . . forgiveness. Not just this Gospel passage, but the entire Gospel is really about forgiveness. And Jesus, by His teaching and by His life, keeps reminding us that forgiveness is the signature of our God and a basic characteristic that everyone who tries to follow our God and be faithful should develop in their life.

But, Peter comes along and he's got a question. And I want to say, "Good question, Peter! Great question! That's exactly what we're all asking." Peter says, "How far do I have to go with this forgiveness stuff?" Peter takes a safe, round number of seven and holds that up as the outside limit, but Jesus answers by giving another number—and a story. And both the number and the story are astonishing!

The number Jesus gives is not seven but 70 times seven. Now, I'm lousy at math so I got my calculator out and that comes to 490 times. That's a lot of forgiving! But, Jesus goes on then to tell a more astounding story. He tells about this kingdom where the king (this is our world where our God is King) finds someone who has a debt to him of 10,000 talents. Now, I'm going to let you figure that one out. It wouldn't fit on my calculator. But scholars tell us that 10,000 talents would be a full day's income (so, think about your own income, a full day's income) multiplied by one hundred million. That's a lot. And the king not only writes that off, but this king demands that every member in our kingdom forgive one another, even in little things like a hundred pennies. Forgiveness. You know, I think the average gum-chewing American and the average gum-chewing Catholic probably wants to say, "You gotta be kidding! You gotta be kidding!" But Jesus says our God is a forgiving God, even in an unforgiving world; and our God calls us to be like that and fashions us to be like that.

I'm going to make just two quick points about forgiveness. One is that it's healthy and the other is that it's not destructive.

The first one is that forgiveness is very healthy. If we're not forgiving, if we keep holding onto hostility, it is not good for us. It is not healthy. Once upon a time, there was a young boy sitting on a park bench, and you could tell by looking at his face that he was in pain. He was in agony. And a man came by and said, "What's the matter?" And the little boy said, "I'm sitting on a bumble bee and it keeps stinging me." And the man said, "Why don't you get up off the bench?" And the little boy said, "I figure I'm hurting him more than he's hurting me." The pain will not stop and the healing will not begin 'til we get up off the bench!

In 1994, the Gallup Institution did an interesting poll. They developed a questionnaire which they called "A Hostility Index." How angry are the people in this community? It asks nine questions, and they identified the five cities in the United States with the highest rate of hostility and anger. The number one city was Philadelphia, the City of Brotherly Love. What was interesting was that those five cities were also the top five in "death by heart attack." They had the highest coronary disease rate in the country. As the director of the Medical Center at Duke University said at the time, "Anger kills." There is a strong correlation between hostility and the death rate. The more angry people are, the shorter their life span. And another doctor involved in the study said, "Grudge-holders are grave diggers, but the only grave they're digging is their own." Now, why do you think that is? I think it's because we are fashioned and shaped by our forgiving God and when we go against that, even if we're not aware of it, the price we pay is enormous! Forgiving is healthy.

Forgiveness is not destructive. Once upon a time, in a small village, a man had a question about forgiveness. He was directed to the wisest, holiest person in the village, an old woman. He went to the old, wise, holy woman and said, "If my neighbor slaps me in the face, should I forgive him?" And she said, "Yes." And he said, "How many times should I forgive him?" And she said, "How many times did he slap you in the face?" He said, "He slapped me once." And she said, "Then, forgive him once." He thought for a moment and then he said, "What if my neighbor should slap me in the face 50 times? How many times should I forgive him?" The wise old woman said, "Forty-nine times." And he said, "Why 49? Why not 50?" She said, "One slap is for your face and you deserve it for being such a fool as to let him do that."

You know, every one of us is called daily both to give forgiveness and to seek forgiveness. That does not mean that forgiveness and returning to business as usual. To be faithful and proactive about forgiving does not mean advocating destructive behavior or unhealthy codependency.

Examples: What if it's not a single incident, but a long pattern of hurtful behavior? What if it's a pattern of being battered, whether physically or emotionally? What if it's being continuously abused? What if it's a serious betrayal? What then? You still forgive, but forgiving does not mean to deny or ignore the hurt. It does not mean returning to the same old relationship and situation. And, it does not mean setting ourselves up as victims. What it does mean—and this is very, very hard—it does mean letting go of the hostility. It does mean foregoing getting even. In fact, that's where the word "forgiveness" comes from. Forgive. Forego. Forego getting even. It does mean trying to be compassionate in our understanding of the other person, but also keeping a healthy sense of our own worth, taking responsibility for ourselves and establishing peace with that other person or with a group as best we can and as safely as we can.

Now, none of this is easy for us. It's not easy for the Church. In fact, I think the Church as an institution has a terrible history of not being good at forgiveness. We're not good at it as a Nation. It's not easy for nations or countries or for our world, but, Jesus says, for those who follow Him, forgiveness is not just a suggestion but a mandate. It's not just an occasional random act, but it should be a characteristic and a quality of our life. It's not just a nice idea, but a basic necessity and a way of living. Why? Jesus says it's because He knows the secret. And He tells us the secret. The secret is that's the way our God is and that's how our God treats us.

Loving and forgiving are You, O Lord.
Slow to anger, rich in kindness.
Loving and forgiving are You.
Amen.

Thanksgiving Day Mass

Homily of November 25, 1999

Last Sunday we began talking about our observance of the Millennium, the "Why," the "Who," and the "What" of the Millennium. The "Why" is Jesus. The "Who" have to be the people for 2000 years, and the "What" is what have we learned along the way, what wisdom and hope to help us to walk into the next century.

Well, here we are at Thanksgiving, and I think what we have to do is give thanks for the people who've gone before us and pay attention to the wisdom and lessons along the way. It's a time to be thankful and also a time to learn. Who are we thankful for? The opening reading was a blend of the Scripture, the Book of Psalms (148), of praising God, and the words from a Grandfather's Prayer, and talking about prayer.

Grandparents. We give thanks for our grandparents. How many here had grandparents? Let's have a show of hands. Who came to the United States from another country? A lot of us, a lot of us. For me, it was my parents, but a lot of us. We give thanks that they came. We wouldn't be here otherwise. And the lesson we have to learn—the wisdom we have to look for—is how do we welcome people? Because in many cases, our grandparents were not welcomed well. How do we treat people who are different from us? Very often, our grandparents who came here were different from our society and were not treated well. We should learn some wisdom from that, about how we welcome others, how we treat others. In my case, it was my father. When he arrived in the United States, one of the first things he saw, and I still have a sign, was "Help Wanted. No Irish Need Apply." Now that was an improvement over the signs that were in England saying, "No Dogs. No Catholics. No

Irish." And in this country, we had our parallel: "No Dogs. No Catholics. No Coloreds." We give thanks for our grandparents and our parents, who came here and dealt with those attitudes. Do we learn something from it and gain wisdom for walking into the next century?

We also give thanks to our ancestors as Americans, like the Puritans, the Pilgrims that we celebrate on Thanksgiving. We should be thankful that they set a kind of standard along the way, a standard that religion was precious to them. Have we learned that? Because that's one of the reasons they came. And for freedom to worship, that everyone's right and freedom to worship, even different from our own, is something precious. And also the willingness to make a change. Look at the change they made. What was it? There were actually two ships that came over with the Pilgrims. One did not make it at all. The other had 102 Pilgrims on it and 51 of them died in the first winter. They faced terrific risk to make a change and to learn from others because they had to learn new ways.

Which brings us to another group to be thankful for, that we don't think of very often, and that's the Native American Indians who met them here and, first of all, *helped* them to survive that first winter. (They would not have lived without them.) Secondly, *celebrated* with them; and, thirdly, (we forget this) but from their customs, among the Algonquian and Huron Indians, *helped fashion the form of democracy* that we took up in America in our U.S. Constitution. It was those Indian tribal leaders who came and addressed, with Benjamin Franklin, our Constitutional Congress. So we have to give thanks for those who went before us and perhaps learn the wisdom and the lesson that, not only do we need to learn from others, but can't we find a way to find our place without having to displace others, which is what we did.

And then we give thanks for ourselves. We want to be thankful, and we want to learn. I'm sure it's in the minds of many today that this has been a fairly difficult year here at Christ the King. And we may think in terms of losses. But I suggest that we should be thinking in terms of blessings. And our memories should bring us wisdom and lessons.

Early in the year, Jim McGee, who I'm very happy is with us celebrating today, left our parish staff, a loss to us, but a blessing. The blessing Jim was to us (a blessing that embarrasses me today) was the blessing of music and of strong leadership at the altar. I can't sing like he did and so you won't be hearing it. And you'll notice, he may start bursting out. But, that's a blessing that we have to count.

Padraig left our staff in March. But the blessing he left was a strong ministry to the divorced, a changed catechumenate, and RCIA. It will never be the same and it will always be better because of him, a blessing.

Our school burned down in May. But think of the blessings of all the years and learnings that went on in that school. One former student wrote from Sacramento how sad he was that the school burned down, because that's where he had sneaked his first kiss, behind the school. I didn't know that was on the curriculum, but there's a great deal of learning and blessings that we can look back on and give thanks for.

Monsignor Wade. We lost him just recently. But the blessing he was and will continue to be, a blessing of dedication, a blessing of holiness, and a blessing that he suggested to us all along, and still does, that we're all still pretty young. He relativized everything for us.

And just recently, the loss of Margo Schorno and the blessing she was, telling us that parish life can be creative and that we need to be connected. I think those were big issues and blessings she shared with us—creativity and connecting us.

We've learned and we give thanks. We will continue to learn, and we will continue to give thanks. Amen.

New Wine in New Wineskins

Homily of February 27, 2000
Based on Luke 5

Some things never change, especially around religious practice. They ask Jesus, "Why don't your disciples fast? Why don't you do things the way we used to do things?" They ask, "Why don't you give up meat on Friday like you used to? Why don't you have a communion rail like we used to in Church? Why don't you have candles? When I was growing up, in Church we had lots of candles. Why don't we have candles in Church? Why don't you have the tabernacle in the center? Why is it off to the side, or in most Catholic churches today, in a different building and in a different place? Why don't you do things the way you used to?"

Now, to questions like this about religious practice, there's always a short-term answer and a big-picture, long-term answer. And Jesus does this. They ask Him why his disciples don't fast. He gives them a short-term answer first. He says, "Well, you know, it's like being in a wedding reception. You're not going to stop eating and drinking 'til the bride and groom leave. Right? You're going to keep it up as long as you can." But, then He gives a long-term answer, "You know, you can't put new wine into old skins. You always have to put new wine into today's skins, into fresh skins."

Short-term answers—Why don't we give up meat on Friday like we used to? Well, we still fast in solidarity with one another and the poor, at times like Ash Wednesday and Good Friday during Lent. But, the point of fasting is to change our hearts. And maybe in another culture and another generation, if the whole town and the whole culture and the whole country had to fast, whether they liked it or not, maybe it changed their hearts.

I don't know. But we know that in our century, in our culture, in our generation, fasting by mandate, en masse and by rote doesn't change anybody's heart. You have to do it personally. You have to make your own decisions.

Communion rails—The short-term answer is, "Well, if you take a house and put a communion rail in the middle of it, it's like two rooms. We've got one room where all the unholy people are and we've got another room where all the holy people are. We're supposed to be a single Eucharistic people gathered around the table of the Lord." That's the short-term answer.

Candles—When it comes to lights and candles in Church, I grew up with lots of candles in Church. The short-term answer is, "Ask your insurance agent."

The tabernacle—The short-term answer is that the tabernacle was invented for emergencies. It was invented so that if somebody was sick and dying and Mass wasn't going on and we couldn't bring communion to them, we had invented a place where the host could be kept for sick and dying emergencies. Also, over the years, it became a place for private prayer, private devotion. Once upon a time, four hundred years ago, when there was a huge argument in the Church about the presence of Jesus in the tabernacle, it seemed to make sense to move it to the center and say, "We're going to make a statement, this year, during this debate." But, we know that today that debate's over and, to put the tabernacle in the center of a Church not only contradicts the rhythm of the Mass where we are gathered and the bread and wine is not yet consecrated, but it also gives the impression that we gather in a temple of private prayer and private devotion when we're supposed to be in a gathering place of all God's people around one Eucharist. Those are the short-term answers.

But there are bigger, long-term questions and answers. For a living, believing, traditional community, values and wisdom and tradition are passed on only when our practices regularly change to best express and best fit today. Or as Jesus put it, you can't put new wine in old wineskins. You need fresh wineskins every day. We have to make kind of an interesting choice. I don't know if you can visualize this because it makes more sense in print. But, if you think of the word "tradition," there's a small "t" which just means "customs." We have the custom of coming to Mass late. That's one of our traditions, right? OK? That's just a small "t." But the big "T" is the Tradition of our wisdom that we don't want to lose. The choice we end up making, is our tradition going to be the dead and buried faith of living people? Or is it going to be living faith of those who went before us? That's what it should be.

Pope John XXIII said that, as a Church, we're not called to be curators of a museum, holding onto precious old items, but we're called to something much messier. We're called to be a living family, passing on values and wisdom and beliefs for today. This is how it works. The specific practices and concrete activities and expressions of our spirituality and of our religion are always necessary. We need that, but they always are and always have been, and always will be subject to change. Think about it. Novenas, rosaries, church architecture, church music, the way we celebrate confessions, the way we celebrate Mass, rules and regulations, styles of Church leadership, exercise of authority, these are always subject to change. What is not subject to change is our values, our wisdom, and our core beliefs! Although, if you watch carefully, you'll notice even our core beliefs and our wisdom and our values look and feel a little different from age to age, because they are not supposed to be left on a shelf to get dusty, but they should be applied to new situations, to address current questions, and to find their flesh in daily lives.

You know, as a parish priest working with people on their spiritual journey, I worry sometimes because I find that there are good Christians and good Catholics who are struggling to keep their faith alive and end up feeling guilty, because they feel they're cheating. They feel they're coming up short. They feel that they are picking and choosing. They get accused of being "Selective Christians" or "Cafeteria Catholics" or are even accused of rejecting the "one true faith." What they are really doing is following today's Gospel and taking the necessary steps to put new wine in fresh wineskins.

There was a very holy and great theologian in the 19th century. You probably know the name, Cardinal John Henry Newman. He taught that to have real faith you need two things and you need them both. One he called "notional assent." It surprises people but he said there are some things in our Creed, things that we list that really in his life didn't make a lot of sense to He. He just said, OK, whatever. If you say so, but I'm not going to think about it. We just give "notional assent" to some things. There are other things to which we give "real assent." We say, "This matters. This makes sense to me. This makes a difference in my life, or it should." And we need both notional and real assent to be true believers.

Over the last three weekends, we've looked at some major figures of the Millennium. And what we've looked at is how did they put together the ancient faith in a living way in their generation. First we looked at Hildegarde of Bingen. And how Hildegarde put together her unique sense of the presence of God and her century's music and art and medicine and its politics and its Church controversy. How did she do that?

Then we looked at Francis and Clare. How did they understand the ancient call to be "poor in spirit?" Poverty and simplicity, how did they put them to work in their century, which was one of commercialism, of exploding wealth, of urbanization and exploding media and new art?

Then we looked at Dorothy Day. How did she take the values of the Gospel and apply them to the labor movement, to homelessness, and to the Second World War, the Korean War, and the Vietnam War?

For Hildegard, her experience of God was a refreshing green presence of God. And she went through her life, and she lived into her eighties, most of the time accepting rules and regulations and authority gladly. But, finally at one point, she ignored all that and she picked a fight, when she found it absolutely necessary, when she found that what was going on was contrary to her experience of God as a refreshing compassionate God.

Francis and Clare came along and wanted to live a life of poverty, and there was a Catholic way of doing that. You go off and become a hermit. But they said, "That doesn't work for our century." So, they banded people together in communities and communes that went traveling and preaching and shared a common poor life. And the Franciscan movement continues to band people together that way today.

Dorothy Day founded a house, the Catholic Worker House in New York, a newspaper and a movement dedicated to justice and compassion. She was often in conflict with the tried and true, the accepted and the authoritative way of being a good Catholic.

What is it we are we talking about? New wine needs fresh wineskins. Otherwise, it's stale wine, and we're not called to that. How do we be a people of Tradition and a living faith. I'd suggest a few steps. One is that we never lightly or easily dismiss the old, even if we don't appreciate it or understand it, lest something very precious and very central be lost or misplaced. Secondly, we keep trying to seek out the true meaning and value behind the words we use, the things we say, the way we celebrate. And finally, we try to apply our wisdom and our belief, not to history and the past, but to daily life and to the present. That's what we're called to do. It ain't easy. We do not always get it right, and often we don't agree with each other.

It's interesting, in the1970s a common comment was made in both Catholic and non-Catholic newspapers about Dorothy Day and William F. Buckley, another Catholic figure who disagreed with her in lifestyle, in politics, in opinion, and in just about everything. The comment being made was, "Isn't it amazing that Dorothy Day and William F. Buckley, both Catholics, can go to the same church, celebrate the same Eucharist, walk down the aisle side by side and receive the same Jesus, and still be united in that, even though they differ over everything else!"

The Eucharist is what holds us together and sends us forth. We don't come to the Eucharist to visit a museum or to enjoy nostalgia or to relive the past. We come to the Eucharist to be challenged and changed together by the living Word of God, to be nourished by the presence of Jesus, and then to go out to live our Faith in a real way in the very real world. Amen.

First Communion

Bulletin Letter — April 28, 2013

It must be First Communion season. Over recent weekends, we've had about 170 children make their First Communion. Believe it or not, this is the smallest number we've had in years, with fewer than the usual six First Communion Masses (although the size of upcoming classes do let us know the numbers will go up next year). May our belief and understanding of Christ's presence continue to deepen and grow up. The Catholic belief and conviction about the real presence of Jesus in Communion finds its foundation in the faith that the Risen Lord is no longer bound by the restraints of time and place. However, that belief stands midway between two extremes which the Church has always rejected.

The first extreme is the understanding that Christ's presence is "merely symbolic" and no more than that. So, the presence of Jesus, if anything, is all in our heads or in our remembering. A second and quite different extreme which the Church also rejects is the view that Jesus is *physically* present, that is, present materially, so that somehow His atoms and molecules hide just beneath the surface of the bread and wine. Sometimes our own vocabulary, with words like "real presence," "substantial presence," and even "physical presence," betrays us into this extreme. Both extremes, "symbolic" and "material," misrepresent Scripture, Tradition, and orthodox Catholic belief.

The authentic Catholic understanding about Christ's presence in Communion can be described in two statements.

1) The presence of Jesus is personal and it is real. It is not the presence of an object or thing, but the personal presence of the Lord. The old *Baltimore Catechism* and its answer that Christ is

present "Body and Blood, Soul and Divinity" was trying to get at that whole, personal presence.

2) Secondly, it is the presence of the Risen and Spirit-filled Christ, not a matter of molecular flesh and body fluids. Christ's Aramaic words at the Last Supper, "This is My body; This is My blood," are more helpfully and accurately put into English as "This is Myself, and this is My life given for you."

Through the centuries from New Testament days, the Church has recognized that the fundamental purpose of Christ's presence is not for Him to be adored and not for our isolated private devotion and piety. The goal and purpose of Christ's presence is to lead us as a Body in a sacrifice of praise to God, our Creator, Father, and Author. Its further purpose is to nourish our lives and to transform us into the community of His Body and to empower that Body, a Eucharistic people, to continue His mission.

This brings us to the real presence of Jesus—not in communion. A funny thing happened to Catholics on their way to Mass. Once upon a time, Catholic Christians at Eucharist, as the New Testament tells us, recognized that Christ was among them as they gathered in His name; as they passed on precious words of Scripture knowing it was a living contact with the person of Jesus; as they recognized Him in the breaking of the bread and celebrated that they were one Body with Him. Somewhere in the Dark and Middle Ages, their attention became almost completely riveted on the host and, whether out of awe or superstition, or no longer understanding the Latin, or a sense of unworthiness, they seldom received communion, but came mainly to watch the host and the chalice held up high.

Then in the 1500s, Catholics understood (in some cases, misunderstood) Protestant reformers to say that Jesus was not really present in communion, but just a symbolic reminder of Him. That really got their dander up. As Catholics went to Mass, they insisted and focused on one thing, to the exclusion of everything else, namely, that Mass produces the real presence of Christ in the consecrated bread and wine and nothing else compares to that, or even much matters. They forgot their own faith in the presence of Christ in the entire celebration of the Eucharist and, in many ways, beyond the Mass. This Eucharistic amnesia led to some strange behavior and consequences. Even though it is Catholic faith that Christ is present as we assemble in His name, and Christ is present as we hear the word of Scripture proclaimed, they were told it's really OK if you miss the entire first part of the Mass (the gathering and Liturgy of the Word). Just be sure to get in before the really important things begin to happen. Hopefully, we've moved well beyond that, as the Second Vatican Council (back in the 1960s) spoke of Christ's presence not only in consecrated bread and wine but also in the proclaimed word and the assembly itself. As one of our official Eucharistic prayers reads: "Blessed too is Your son, Jesus Christ, who is present among us and whose love gathers us together. As once He did for His disciples, Christ now opens the Scriptures for us and breaks the bread."

Pope Paul VI in his encyclical letter on the Eucharist reaffirmed belief in the presence of Christ in communion, but he also spoke of the very real presence of Christ in acts of concern and compassion, in the preaching of God's word, in the faithful shepherding of God's people, and in the celebration of all the sacraments. Christ comes to us in many ways, but the Mass (not one magic moment, but the Mass from beginning to end), is the principal and most important way he touches us, nourishes us, calls and causes us to be His Body and sends us out to make a difference in our world.

Mother's Day

Homily of May 14, 2000

The preacher who dares to get up and speak on Mother's Day faces at least three problems or dangers. And they are all the more acute in the Catholic Church because, more often than not, the preacher is male and unmarried. The three dangers I am speaking of are the danger of "being an expert," the danger of using Mary as the model of motherhood, and the danger of facing a very mixed congregation.

The danger of being an expert: You all know the story of the priest who got up and spoke at great length on the glories of motherhood. And when he walked outside a woman came up to him and said, "Father, I wish I knew as little about being a mother as you do." Or the other priest who preached about Mary as the perfect model to be a wife and mother. And a woman came up to him, carrying one baby and with four other children following her and said, "It was easy enough for her with her one child."

And then, our congregation is mixed. We celebrate Mothers' Day. We talk about and honor mothers. And yet many in our congregation are not mothers, are not married, and are not women. What we all have in common is that we've all had a mother. We've all had the experience of a mother.

Two verbs come to my mind when I think about the experience of being raised and growing up and becoming an adult and, in my case, letting go of a mother. The first verb is to *treasure*. We treasure the memories, the importance, the impact and the love of our mothers. The second verb is to *forgive* because, despite what it says on the Hallmark Greeting Cards, mothers are not perfect, and they should not be expected to be perfect and they are never going to be perfect. Now what that does is, later on as we go through life, sometimes, it's gentle and we just look back and smile. You see the foldout on today's bulletin, a lot of quotes about mothers and things they said. My favorite thing my mother always said to me was, "Shut your mouth and eat your food." This always had me just a little confused. I still am! But, in some cases, we look back and there were hurts, and it takes time to heal. And there were resentments, and it takes time to forgive.

It's interesting that Jesus is always trying to give us a peek at what God is like. Opening little windows, ways of looking at God to make sure our notion of God keeps getting cleaned up again and again. In today's Gospel, He talks about God as a shepherd and Himself as a shepherd, the Good Shepherd. I don't think it's because God is primarily in the sheepherding profession, but there is something about a caring, give-my-life-to-defend-my-sheep shepherd that tells us something about God.

I remember the first time I went to the Holy Land, to Israel, the Land of the Good Shepherd was with a group of around fifty parishioners from Christ the King. We arrived in the evening and got to a hotel in Tiberius, we got up the next morning, the sun rising on the Sea of Galilee. We went by bus to visit Capernaum, and then to the Mount of the Beatitudes and celebrated Mass there. On our way back, we were going by bus and there was a beautiful field of red poppies. In the middle of it was a shepherd, my first real-life Israeli, Palestinian, like-Jesus, Good Shepherd, just as I had imagined. The shepherd was standing there, with his back to me, caring for the sheep, staff in hand, surrounded by these little sheep, the perfect image of what Jesus was talking about. The bus came around the corner, and I saw it was a woman. Women shepherds! Is that what Jesus was talking about?

Well, you notice in the first reading, that special creed for Mothers' Day, we're told our God holds us in Her arms and shelters us under the shadow of Her wings. There's a good pedigree for talking that way. Pope John Paul II did it on several occasions. The *Catholic Catechism* says if you want to know what God is like you have to look at masculine, at feminine, and more than that. So, let's do that for a moment.

Think about what mothers are like, what our mother was like, not just when we were babies or between age one and five, but through our entire life. Three things strike me about the experience of being mothered. First of all, our mother makes life possible and gives us the gift of life. Secondly, particularly as we grow up, our mother does not control us but tries to persuade us all the time. She's always trying to persuade us, sometimes successfully, sometimes unsuccessfully, but she never has complete control as we're growing up. Finally, our mother has to let go and hope for the best!

That's the kind of God we have. Sometimes God shows a masculine mood, but more often, a feminine face. That's very faithful to the Bible. Not all lines in the Bible are like that. But that's certainly an image of the God of the Prophets, a vulnerable God whom we find in the Bible, a God of the weak and lowly, a God of the crucified, a God of the Pieta, a God who hides power and empties self on our behalf.

So now think about your own image and feeling about the Creator, the God of the Universe, the God of all the Galaxies and Planets, if you will, and the God of weather, storm and earthquake. Think about the God of all people, all men and women, all children, everyone, good and bad, saints and sinners, criminals and non-criminals (which means, those of us who haven't been caught yet). If we take the experience of Mother that we all have and say that's a window into what God is like, we realize that God, despite what we were raised with, is less a God of control than we thought. God is not primarily a Great Designer and the Great Planner, but rather the God who tries to persuade us but lets us go.

Think about our whole world as God's children, our whole Universe, both the physical world and its people. If we're all God's children and we're like all children, there are a few things about us we need to be aware of. One, as we grow up we are self-organizing. Think of the Universe as self-organizing. As we grow up we are unpredictable. Think of the Universe as unpredictable. As we grow up, we are full of promise. Think of God's Universe as full of promise. And where is God in all of this? God is that loving Ground of our being, who makes it possible, who's always persuading us, and who lets us go.

May God who is neither male nor female, but both Father and Mother and much more, bless us all, the God who holds us in Her everlasting arms and gathers us protectively under the shelter of Her wings, who binds our wounds, dries our tears, and promises better things. Amen.

The Essentials of Parish Life

Homily of July 2, 2000

In the coming week, we celebrate the 4th of July and give thanks for a lot of blessings in our Land. One of them is freedom of worship, freedom of religion. So, I thought it might be worthwhile to reflect just a little bit about what it is that we do with our religion, what it is that we are about. A congressman from Massachusetts, Tip O'Neil, used to say, "All politics are local." Well, I'd also say, "All religion is local." Our experience of religion, our experience of church, is local. It's not in Rome. It's in Pleasant Hill. So the question to ask, if we want to know what we do about our religion is to reflect on, "What is parish all about? What is parish life all about?" I want you to think about that for a few seconds. If you had to list two or three things that are essential to a parish life, what would they be?

Just last month, I read a journal from Chicago (It comes out four times a year.) and they had a big article on parish life. The guy who wrote it listed two things essential to parish life. I'm going to disagree with him a little bit. So you think about, "What's essential to parish life? What two or three or four things?" I'll probably disagree with you too. So make your list in your own minds. Here are his. He says, "There are two things that are essential to parish life, our Pastoral Care and Evangelization." My first reaction, this list is too short.

My list has four on it. Number one, basic and essential to parish life, is Community. I mean, you can be a hermit by yourself, but you can't be a parish by yourself. Maybe, all by yourself, you can be a saint, although, I think, a pretty mean-spirited one. But you couldn't be a parish. All by yourself, you could be an isolated Messiah, which is the most dangerous kind of Messiah. But you can't be a parish. Parish is a community. It's a community of people knit together by faith and by the word of God. That's the first thing. We have all sorts of things. That's what they're about in our parish life, for example, our school, our adult education, our small church communities, our coffee and donuts after Mass. They all have to do with the fact that, number one, we're a community knit together by the word of God.

Number two. (I'm amazed the author of the article didn't have this.) Maybe it's on your list of things basic and essential to parish life. Number two is worshiping God, praising God, with Jesus, usually in the Eucharist. We're called to be a Eucharistic community, not a club, not a fraternity, not a circle of friends, but a worshipping community together. So I have that down as number two.

Now, three and four. That's all I've got. Three and four are the ones the guy from Chicago used. Pastoral Care, yeah, I think so. When we listen to the gospel today, Jesus is healing this woman. One scene after the other, it's Jesus healing and bringing hope to people. So, that's what we have to be about. She touched the hem of His garment. In a way, a parish community has to be the hem of Christ's garment for this day and age. And, that's what we do in parish life all the time, our bereavement ministry, our visiting of the sick, our counseling, our St. Vincent de Paul Society, and each one of you individually reaching out to someone who needs help. That's Pastoral Care. It's the third thing we're about.

Now, here's the fourth one. He says it's "Evangelization." I wrote down "Evangelization" and put in parentheses, "It depends . . . . It depends." Think, for a moment, what you mean by "Evangelization." When you hear the word, what picture or image do you get in your mind? I want to ask you that, because there is a Catholic definition of evangelization that popes and bishops and all those fancy people talk about, that's what they are referring to. When you hear "Evangelization," what do you hear? What do you mean?

Here's the Pope's definition. When a Catholic says "Evangelization" this is what we're supposed to mean. "Evangelization is bringing the Good News into every level of humanity and, through its influence, not by baptizing or converting anybody, but through its influence, transforming humanity from within and making it new." That's what we mean. But I gotta tell you the problem is it may work in other countries and in other languages, but, in English, in the United States of America, somebody else has the copyright on the word "Evangelization." And so, when we hear the "Evangelization," we say Fundamentalists. We say proselytizing. We say going around knocking on people's doors to tell them about Jesus and to irritate them. We say TV evangelists, TV curers, TV preachers asking for money. That's what Evangelization brings to mind for us, but it's not what we mean when we use it in our Church. A better word might be the "Mission of the Church," "Outreach of the Church." And we find it throughout the gospels.

St. Paul, in the second reading, is talking about equality for everyone. That's one of the values we have to stand behind. Jesus talks about feeding the poor, clothing the naked, visiting the imprisoned, that kind of outreach! It's bringing values and wisdom and justice to the world. So, when we say "Evangelization," we're not supposed to be thinking about the Church at all. "Evangelization" doesn't mean, "How well is the Church doing?" or "How many people does the Church have?" or "How lively is the Church?" or "How strong is the Church getting?" It's not about that at all. It's about the world. It's about society around us, because that's the location where God's will is going to work or not. That's the location of God's Kingdom on earth. And the role of the parish, the role of the Church, is just to bring some energy, some values, some support and some celebration to the life of our society and of our world.

So, here are a few questions. Was the 4th of July a Church event? Was the Declaration of Independence a Church event? If you mean "Evangelization," the answer is absolutely yes.

Was the Emancipation of slaves in our nation a Church event? Absolutely, yes. Was the Suffrage Movement for women's vote a Church event? Was the gathering of the United Nations a Church event? Is the Declaration of Human Rights by the U.N. a Church event? If you mean "Evangelization," absolutely . . . absolutely!

The Bishops of the world met in Europe in 1970 and tried to define what it means to be proclaiming the Gospel, because that's something we're supposed to be about. Right? They said working for justice is the constitutive part of proclaiming the Gospel. If we're not working for justice as a parish, then the Gospel's not being proclaimed. It's tough to work out what justice is sometimes. That's why bringing a dynamic speaker and Scripture scholar from Berkeley, and she'll be talking about the question of justice in the Bible. We invite you to join us on two Tuesday nights. Keep that in mind.

I'm gonna finish with just one quote. It's from a big Church document, written by almost 3,000 bishops and the Pope in 1965. I'm not big on Church documents. Here's my problem with them. I start reading them and then I fall asleep. You know, there's something about Church documents. They've got sleeping pills built into them. But, fortunately, these great lines on the Church and the World were at the beginning, the first paragraph. So, I got that far. And it talks about what the Church is about and what we, as a parish, are supposed to be about. Here's what it says, "The joys and hopes, the griefs and anxieties of the people of this age, especially those who are poor and those who are afflicted in any way, these too are the joys and hopes, the griefs and anxieties, of those who follow Jesus." That's us! "Indeed, nothing genuinely human fails to raise an echo in our hearts. This community—" (Roman Catholic Church, this community Christ the King Parish; this community . . .)—"realizes that it is truly and intimately linked with humanity at every level and in all its history." Wow!

So, as a parish, we are called to be gathered as a community of faith, to worship God in a spirit and the presence of Jesus Christ, to care for one another, and finally, I don't care what you call it, "Evangelization," if you want, or "mission," we're called to work for fully human values and true justice everywhere in our world. That's the spirit of St. Paul, calling for equality. It's the spirit of Jesus, bringing healing and hope to people. It's the spirit of the 4th of July that talks about independence, freedom and justice for all. Amen.

The Many Faces of Forgiveness - Ten Commandments

Homily of March 4, 2001
Based on Luke 4:1-13

First weekend of Lent, and my reaction is, "Same old . . . same old . . . same old." Every time, we begin Lent with the same story, in different versions, of Jesus being tempted by the Devil out in the desert. Christ is tempted to seize power, to pursue fame, to take a quick easy fix and a quick easy way to proclaim the Gospel of God. Instead, He chooses the way of a servant, the way of plodding, the way of faithful working through it, the way of sticking to the values of God's Kingdom, even if it leads to His death.

I think the choice of this Scripture at the beginning of every Lent is telling us that Lent is a good time for us to reflect on those values and issues of the Kingdom of God's wisdom and ways, that we have to work at, that we have to plod at, that we have to stick to, that we have to work through. And one of those is very clearly "forgiveness." So, during this season of Lent, our parish community, every weekend, will be reflecting on the many faces of "forgiveness."

Now, we didn't choose this because of Bill Clinton and the pardons that he's given. No. Uh - Uh! The very signature of trying to be a follower of Jesus is *forgiveness*. Jesus calls us to work at forgiveness. And, in that, Jesus is different from all the other world religions and all other leaders. Jesus says, "Forgive your enemies." Moses says, "An eye for an eye." Jesus says, "Forgive your enemies." Confucius says that forgiveness violates justice. Jesus says, "Forgive your enemies." Mohammed says you can use force against your enemies. Buddha says deal with what's inside, your inner peace, let the outside relationships take care of themselves. And Jesus says, "No. You take care of them."

Forgive one another. We are called to be a people of forgiveness. And it is not only our signature as a community, it is also one of our most common difficulties and most constant challenges. Brothers and sisters in the same family have fights, and sometimes they go on for years, and they can't forgive each other. Spouses sometimes hurt one another and find it very hard to really forgive. Friends disappear out of our lives, because of a word said. Coworkers hurt us, and we find it hard to forgive.

Even communities have the same problem. This is why John Paul II, last year, publicly asked for forgiveness from the women who had been abused by the Church, the Jews who had been abused by the Church, members of the Church who had been abused by the Church, and all those whose human rights had been abused in history by the Church. Jesus says in today's Gospel, "You do not live by bread alone." But, if we don't have the bread of forgiveness, we cannot be whole and healthy human beings. And as a community without the bread of forgiveness, we don't really deal with one of our major tasks as a Church, which is to make credible the power of forgiveness in human affairs.

So, what I have done is I have put together "ten commandments of forgiveness." Now, you are not going to remember all of them, but some of them might strike a chord with you. And you don't have to take any notes, because I am going to put them in the Bulletin next weekend. And, like the Commandments of Moses, the first few are negative. It's not this. It's not that. It's not the other thing. The later ones are positive. So, here we go.

Ten Commandments of Forgiveness:

The First Commandment is: *Forgiveness is not easy*. There is no cheap grace. There is no quick fix. A mother says to her child, "Tell him you're sorry". . . . "I'm sorry." That doesn't mean a thing. If it's quick and easy it's not real. Forgiveness is not easy.

The Second Commandment: *Forgiveness is not forgetting.* We say, "Forgive and forget." Baloney! Baloney! Forgiveness is about a change of heart, not a bad memory or having a senior moment. Forgiveness is not forgetting.

The Third Commandment: *Forgiveness does not overlook evil.* It doesn't mean that we accept injustice or naively pretend that all is well, when it isn't. It doesn't mean denial. It doesn't mean, "Let's pretend." Forgiveness does not overlook evil.

The Fourth Commandment: *Forgiveness is not destructive.* What that means is where things are harmful and wrong, it doesn't just go back to "business as usual, let the hurt and damage go on." Forgiveness is not destructive.

The Fifth Commandment: *Forgiveness is not the same thing as approval.* We can be forgiving and, at the same time, express our disagreement, express our disapproval of harmful behavior.

Those are the first five. I'm going faster than Moses did. And they are all negative. Forgiveness is not easy. Forgiveness is not forgetting. Forgiveness does not overlook evil. Forgiveness is not destructive. Forgiveness is not the same thing as approval.

Here are the next five:

The Sixth Commandment: *Forgiveness is based on recognizing and admitting that people are always bigger than their faults.* People are always larger and they are more than their mistakes or their wrongdoings. In other words, I don't define somebody and who they are by something they said to me. They are bigger than that. Forgiveness is based on recognizing and admitting that people are always bigger than their faults and their mistakes.

The Seventh Commandment: *Forgiveness is willing to allow a person who has offended us to start over again.* You know, the more common thing is saying, "Never again! No way! I will never let that happen. I will never have anything to do with him again. No way!" Forgiveness means letting go of that. Forgiveness is willing to allow a person who has offended us to start over again.

The Eighth Commandment: *Forgiveness recognizes the humanity of the person who has wronged us and also recognizes our own humanity, our shortcomings and our contributions to what went wrong.*

The Ninth Commandment: *Forgiveness surrenders the right to get even.* Now, isn't that really common? "Boy! I'm going to get you back." "Payback time!" "Revenge!" Or, at least, "Someday you'll be sorry." It means letting go of that and saying: Forgiveness surrenders the right to get even.

And, finally, the Tenth Commandment: *Forgiveness means we wish the person well who hurt us, or the group that hurt us; in fact, we wish them the best.*

During this Lent, as we reflect as a parish community, on the many faces of forgiveness, may we resist the temptation to hold onto hurts. During this Lent, may we fast from anger and resentment. During this Lent, may we feast on the bread of forgiveness. Amen.

The Prodigal Son . . . And Then What Happened?

Homily of March 25, 2001
Based on Luke 15:11-31

"The Many Faces of Forgiveness," the Season of Lent, and the Gospel give us symbols and stories to help us follow Jesus. Symbols such as the *loaf of bread* from the first Gospel of Lent where Jesus said, "Man does not live by bread alone." The *white robe* that reminds us of the Transfiguration, that we're called to be transfigured and transformed, the *barren fig tree*, reminding us of the story Jesus shared with us last week, and the symbol of *a banquet* given for the Prodigal Son.

The story of the Prodigal Son is a good one, and I always feel one good story deserves another. Besides that, I always wondered what happened with this family the next day. I mean, it was a little shaky right there. So, to find out what happened the next day, I sat down six years ago and wrote what happened. I'd like to share it with you today.

"The Prodigal Son . . . And Then What Happened?"

The day after the party, things went back to normal. The younger son was delighted to be home and delighted with the welcome he had received. His mom and dad were delighted to have the family together again. Things went back to normal, with one big exception. That exception was the older brother. He grew silent, sullen and angry. He worked as hard as ever. In fact, he worked even harder than before. He helped everyone, but it was a stern and severe kind of help. He had wrapped himself in a shroud of cold and unforgiving silence. This went on, not just for a few days, but for years!

Then, one hot summer day, the two brothers found themselves working side by side under the blazing sun, digging holes for a row of new fence posts. It was something they had not done for years; something they had last shared with good humor, cheerful banter, and brotherly horseplay to ease the task. The younger son remembered, and began to cry.

"What's your problem?" snarled his brother.

"I've ruined everything," he said. "I'm sorry! I'm so sorry!"

"Well, you should be."

Then, the younger man shared the story of his days away from home, of how bitter, lonely and frightening it had been.

"Serves you right," his brother grunted. Then, the older brother angrily told his story of how it had been at home, how no matter how hard he tried, nothing could help; nothing could heal the hurt. "The pain in Mom's and Dad's eyes, that was the worst thing, the pain in their eyes. The whole deal was so unfair! You waltzed back home and they gave you a party!" He, too, began to sob. They were tears of anger, but tears nonetheless.

"Forgive me," his brother pleaded.

"I can't," was his reply. "I can't!"

Then, as he turned from his brother, half-blinded by tears and anger, his foot caught in one of the holes they had just dug. The crack of broken bone split the air. At first, the older brother insisted he could hobble the two miles back to home, "Without any help from you, thank you very much!" He didn't need anyone, least of all his younger brother. But hot sun, broken bone, and a rough road soon wrote a different story.

Well over an hour later, the two brothers came staggering home, one half carrying the other, both laughing, joking, and crying in turns. For the first time in years, the younger had helped the older. And, for the first time anyone could remember, the older brother let himself be helped.

A few days later, the father commented to his neighbor, "My son who was dead has come back to life."

"I know," said the neighbor, "you already told us."

The father smiled and his eyes twinkled. "No, no . . . my
other son, the one who never left us, the one who was always
so good, the one who never disobeyed and never got into
trouble, the one who worked so hard and never missed church
on Sunday. He's finally learned how to forgive, and he's finally
learned how to be forgiven. That son was dead. That son was
dead . . . and he has come back to life."

And now you know the rest of the story!

Three Ways to Pray

Homily of July 29, 2001
Based on Luke 11:1-13

Today's Gospel and first reading are all about prayer. One of the more significant theologians of the twentieth century, Charlie Brown, spoke about prayer. He was standing next to Lucy with his hands pointed down and said, "I've made a theological discovery. I found out that if you pray with your hands like this, instead of like this, you get the exact opposite of what you asked for." How many of us have had that experience?!

Another significant theologian in the twentieth century was Father Michael Dibble, who said, "Pray like a pest. Give Jesus no rest!" And that's pretty much what these Scripture readings are about. Pray like a pest. Give Jesus no rest! Although my own experience, and I'll bet some of you will share this with me, is that we tend to pray in spurts. We're not that steady at it. So, I'm going to talk to you, not about when we should pray, but something about how we pray. And I'm going to use a homely division of three kinds of prayer.

The first kind of prayer is *recited* or *memorized prayer*. In the last twenty or thirty years, it has gotten a bad name. And there is something to that. Whereas it is great to pray someone else's prayer, especially the Our Father, the Gloria, the Psalms from the Old Testament, it shouldn't become automatic, and it shouldn't become impersonal, like a parrot reciting something memorized, or a robot. We should use our own words.

That's well and good, but let me say something in favor of memorized, recited prayers. I don't know about you, but it's very hard to get up each day and compose a new prayer. It's very hard to be that spontaneous and creative to always be creating a new prayer with our God. There are ways of doing it, but it's not always that easy. Sometimes, it's easier to hitchhike on somebody else's prayer, rather than to walk alone. But we do need to revitalize those prayers, lest they become dead air, dead weight, and empty phrases. Some people do this. At least once a year, they take one of those prayers that they usually say and they write it out in longhand to reflect on. Others take, maybe once every couple of months, a phrase from a prayer, like "Thy will be done," and spend some time thinking through, "What does that mean in our world today?" Does it even work? Or, "Forgive us as we forgive others." Spend some time around that. Or, "Lead us not into temptation and deliver us from evil." What about evil in the world? How is that working? So, what my suggestion is about memorized and recited prayers is that we do say a prayer every day, at least once a day, and we occasionally try to revitalize those prayers.

The second kind of prayer is the prayer that we least think of as *personal prayer*, and it's the prayer of the gathering. It's a prayer when we gather as an assembly. It's a prayer when we come together, but our language betrays us. We say things such as, "We're going to Mass," or "We hear Mass." We think of ourselves almost as an audience, watching somebody else do the praying, as if it were a spectator sport. And yet it is our most common kind of prayer. But, for it to work, it's not enough just to show up. It doesn't become prayer for you if you just show up. It needs the discipline of participation. And it is a discipline. It means we have to bring energy and bring attention to what we do. It means the discipline of setting aside our own preferences and our biases. It may not be the way that we would choose to pray on a given day. And, yet, with the assembly and gathering, we end up stretching more than we normally would. We end up singing songs, and we might say, "That wouldn't have been my choice today, to sing that song." Or we may end up singing, and that may not be my choice either. I would prefer to be silent. But, if I join in that discipline of participation, prayer of the gathering, I also hear readings that I wouldn't have chosen, reflections on the readings that I might never have heard before or might not even fully agree with, time of silence that I might not have given or set aside, and greeting other people that I would hardly have done on my own.

If we have that discipline of participation and bring energy to our prayer of gathering, then there are moments . . . not every Sunday, not every time, not all the time . . . but there are moments that really touch our hearts and lift our spirits. And when that happens . . . it might be at the Elevation. It might be a phrase from the Gospel. It might be during the greeting of peace with each other. It might be at Communion time. God help us!! It might even be during the homily! (Maybe if we are sitting there thinking of something else, it will happen.) But, if that happens to you, I suggest that, later on in the day, you sit down for five minutes and really think about it, and relish it. Otherwise, we don't anchor that memory and it's just forgotten. And secondly, if we do that, it raises our radar and our antenna, so we are alert for it to happen more and more often.

OK. Two kinds of prayer: recited and memory, and prayer of the gathering. The third kind of prayer I call *"prayer from the heart."* I do this when I'm delighted. I do this when I'm in need. Most of us occasionally give thanks to God, and lots of times we are asking for something, as was Abraham in the first reading, bargaining with God. Sometimes people call that "prayer of embarrassment," because we never think about God. We don't pray, until something happens. Someone gets sick. We pray for them. We lose our job. We pray about it. We buy a lottery ticket. We're not sure it's going to work this time. We pray about it. We don't need to be embarrassed. Jesus tells us our God is a generous God who walks with us and cares for us. We need not be embarrassed.

But we need to do two things. Be a little bit more clear on our notion of God and a little more clear on the notion of ourself, when it comes to the prayer of the heart. Our notion of God: Let me tell you something! Growing up, when I was really young, I really think my notion of God was, first of all, of an angry judge, a co-disciplinarian with my parents, a God who, my mother would say, "You behave yourself or God will punish you." That was my first notion of God, an angry judge. I got over that. I heard about God being a God of love, of unconditional love, a God of mercy, a God of compassion. And then I ended up with a God who was kind of a pushover God. Doesn't matter. Whatever I want, whatever I ask, it's all right with God, a pushover God. And then I think I moved to kind of an absent God. I think of this as "God as the Cosmic Bellhop." You know what a bellhop is like. A bellhop is someone who has nothing to do with us, nothing to do with our life, doesn't even know our name, but, on occasion when we have a big suitcase and it needs to be lifted, steps in and lifts it. So I had that notion of God, nothing to do with my daily life, but if I really needed something, call Him in to lift the baggage.

Jesus gives us a different notion of God, and we should be clear about it. The notion of God Jesus gives us is Our God is a loving parent (now watch this!), a loving parent of grown up adults, not a fairy godmother of little children. And I think we make that mistake. We think God is this parent of little children. We're not little children. And our world is not a child's playground. But our God is the loving parent, like a woman sweeping the house to find a little penny (that's us; our God looks for us); like a shepherd going after one sheep and leaving the other ninety-nine (God is that loving); like a Prodigal Father of the Prodigal Son, who welcomes him back and parties with him (that kind of loving parent). But, you notice, the Prodigal Father had a grown-up son who, when it was time to go and wanted to go, couldn't stop him. When he put himself in danger, couldn't do anything about it. I would like to suggest there are times in our world and in our lives—it might be sickness; it might be a layoff; it might be divorce; it might be an earthquake, or tragedy in the world—where all that our God can possibly do is grieve with us. Not a fairy godmother, but a loving parent of grown-up children. So we have to be clear on our notion of God, when we pray from the heart.

And we also have to be clear about ourselves. Sometimes I'm angry, sometimes I'm delighted, and sometimes I'm needy. That should be coming through in my prayer. It just comes down to being yourself and being real when you pray. Someone once described to me an imaginary scene of the Last Judgment when God says, "I'm glad you're here. I know you said your prayers, but why did you leave so much out? You never mentioned what was really going on in your life. You gave me a lot of stuff out of your brain and nothing out of your heart. You weren't ever real."

Another significant theologian of the twentieth century wrote, I think, a very real prayer. Her name is Erma Bombeck. "Please, God, have I ever called on You for a real biggie? When my washer overflowed, I just offered to build an ark. When I burned the First Communion breakfast, didn't I just laugh? Now, all I'm asking, before I go into the room filled with the reunion class of 1949, is to make me look thin! You can do it. You are the only one who can do it. Do you know what it's like to suck in your stomach and have nothing move? Please, God, dim the lights, crush me in the crowd, and, if you can't make me thin, Lord, on such short notice, could You please make Eloise look fat?" Now, that's a real prayer. And that's not a plaster saint prayer. It's not a model mystic prayer. But it's real!

We, ourselves, whether it's recited prayer from memory, or prayer of the gathering, or prayer from the heart, we need to be ourselves. We need to be real. And we need to give thanks to the Lord who is so good. Amen.

The Eight Flavors of Our Faith

Homily of February 10, 2002

"You are the salt of the Earth."

Some of us have a problem with that. My doctor tells me to lay off of the salt. And health experts tell us that salt is not good for us. And many of us spend a lot of time looking for low-sodium products and salt substitutes.

Obviously, Jesus does not mean "salt." What He means is "flavor." He says that those who follow Him and let their lives be shaped by the values and wisdom of the Gospel should make a difference in the world, should bring a different flavor to the people, the situations, the relationships, the world around them. Now, what flavor is it? If you had to name the flavor, what would you say? I think a lot of Christian people would immediately say "love." I don't think so, first of all, because there are too many different kinds of love. There's parental love. There's romantic love. There's tough love. There's unconditional love. There's limited love. There's friendship love. And there's love that means, "I like my pets." There are all kinds of likes and loves. And also, it's too easy to say, too easy to deal with, like a Hallmark card on Valentine's Day. That should take care of that flavor. So I don't think "love" is good enough. I think it needs at least . . . that salt that we are to be, that flavor that we are to give to the world, has to be broken down. So, today I am going to try to give you a spiritual or a religious visit to Baskin and Robbins. I am going to share with you eight flavors that I think are the flavors of the Gospel that we are supposed to be digesting and giving as a taste and difference to the world around us.

The first flavor is CONCERN. It has to begin there, that we look beyond ourselves, that we are a people who are not concerned just with me, myself, and I, with my things, my family, my neighborhood, my church, or my country . . . that we are a people who look beyond. So, the first flavor that we need to bring to the world, as Gospel people, is concern. And the second flavor is close to that. The second one is COMPASSION. Now the Gospel talks about compassion a lot. In fact, it says, "You need to be compassionate, just as your God is compassionate." But, let me tell you. I think the challenge to be compassionate means mainly with people who are different from us, and people who are close to us. People who are different . . . . You see, if someone is the same as I . . . looks like me, acts like me and has the same opinions as I do, I don't need compassion. All I need is self-interest. All I have to do is like myself. I don't think that's the flavor we are talking about. It comes to bear, we need this flavor when people differ with us, and are different from us. Secondly, not just people who are so distant that we have nothing to do with and can do nothing about, but people who are close enough (and they are all over the world) . . . people who are close enough that we can do something. Otherwise, who cares? So, the second flavor is compassion.

The third flavor is JUSTICE. By justice, I don't mean "fair is fair" or "even-steven." I don't mean "tit for tat." John McCutcheon, the folk singer, has a great line in one of his songs: "It's an easier road to revenge than to mercy. But an eye for an eye leaves the whole world blind . . . . It's an easier road to revenge than to mercy. But an eye for an eye leaves the whole world blind." Justice means to set about right relationships in love. In practice, I think that means it calls on us to be a people who want to bring the flavor in the world, that those who have gifts, and those who have things to share are responsible. And those who are wrong-doers are held accountable. That every human being has their basic needs met, and that everyone has the opportunity to grow and to prosper, not a guarantee, but an opportunity. Now, if we look at the world around us, that's not the situation. That's not the structure. And we have to bring a different kind of flavor. I want to mention, the eight flavors I am going to share with you (I'm up to number three). I do not include peace. I do not think that is one of the flavors. I think it is here. As Pope Paul VI said, "If you want peace, work for justice." The flavor we have to bring is justice.

Number four is FORGIVENESS, forgiveness that is not easy, forgiveness that doesn't just mean, "Forget about it," forgiveness that does not allow injustice to continue. Forgiveness that genuinely recognizes that people are larger than their particular mistakes and larger even than their deliberate faults, and also generously and wisely recognizes our own need, for our own welfare. To have the ability to let go of anger and resentment and hatred and hard hearts. So, those are the first four flavors: concern, compassion, justice and forgiveness.

Here come four more. Number five is INTEGRITY. We need integrity especially in small things, because small things quickly and easily become large, large, large things. We need integrity. I can give one example of small things becoming very large, in one word, Enron . . . Enron. We need integrity.

Number six . . . number six . . . . I think this is the most church-y, religious, spiritual of my eight flavors. HUMOR. We need a sense of humor, because humor is the closest thing to that wisdom and insight that we call faith. You tell somebody a joke and they don't get it . . . . Do you get it? Same thing with faith . . . . Do you get it? Do you have the insight to get what's really going on? Someone has said it is also necessary to be fully human. In fact, of all our creatures, who we reverence and honor on our planet, the only one that laughs and cries is the human being, because we can see the difference between what is and what ought to be. We have to be a people who get it. And a sense of humor also produces a mellow and grateful spirit that leads to thanksgiving and even to Eucharist.

Number seven, the seventh flavor, as Gospel people, that we are called to share with one another and with the world is CREATIVITY. We have to have imagination, the ability to envision and the ability to dream. Didn't Jesus have that? The ability to move beyond where we are and leap into the future, rather than to let relationships that we may be stuck in, situations we may not approve of, or a world that needs to be in a different place . . . . rather than let that become a blind alley or a hopeless road block. In fact, what creativity does, that flavor, it leads to hope.

The eighth and last flavor is JOY, my favorite flavor, joy. Actually it isn't. My favorite flavor is humor. Joy is my second favorite. And it means zest and enthusiasm for life, for creation, for people that signals a thankful heart, a spirit that gives praise. And it leads to love.

So there they are, the eight flavors of the Gospel: concern, compassion, justice, forgiveness, integrity, and humor that leads to faith, creativity that leads to hope, and joy that leads to love. Make no mistake about it. This is a tough message. This is a very hard saying. Remember what Jesus says, if we lose our flavor, what we are good for.

I have a poem that is filled with delightful images, but also a stern, tough reminder. It may not be classic in its form, but I think it is pure Gospel:

You are the salt of the earth, the salt of the earth . . . the salt. Or you are the cheese on hot apple pie, the Worcestershire sauce on steak. You, says Jesus, are the fizz in a coke and the nuts in an Almond Joy. You are the alligator on a shirt's pocket, or, O Christian, a new girdle's stretch. You are the orange glaze on a clay pot, the scent in a grove of pine. Christian, you are the fiddle at the country dance. But what if the salt of the earth loses its saltiness? Or what if the fizz fizzles out, you say, or if the elastic loses its stretch? What if those things lose their stuff, their tang, their shine? "Well," says Jesus, "then you can just call them junk."

Amen.

Retirement

Bulletin Letter — February 24, 2013

What I like to call the forbidden "R word" is suddenly getting a great deal of attention and publicity in the press, on TV, and even on Twitter, all because Pope Benedict XVI has announced his retirement as of February 28th. Actually church law requests pastors who have completed their 75th year to submit their resignation, which may or may not be accepted. Among my classmates I am the only one not to have retired. At a recent clergy gathering, I was advised by one classmate to "follow the example of Pope Benedict." My response was, 85 seems like about the right age for retirement. As a matter of fact, Msgr. Wade, who preceded me here at Christ the King, retired at the age of 82 and then lived with us as a very active priest for twelve more years. With all that in mind, I consider retirement the forbidden "R word," but I still have sent in the following letter for our personnel director.

"As asked for by Canon 528 paragraph 3, of Pastors having completed their 75th year, I am hereby submitting my resignation, although at the same time I have no intention or desire to resign or retire at this time. I feel my health is more than adequate and I am willing and more than capable to continue to serve as pastor here at Christ the King. My intention is to review this on a regular basis and let you now the moment I no longer am able to continue well as pastor. When that time comes, which I trust will be several years off, my intention is to give you at least six months' notice so you can plan appropriately for a successor here at Christ the King."

On Friday evenings during Lent, we continue to feature sensational speakers and delightful soups, and the exact time continues to shift on us. This Friday night the soup supper as usual will be at 6:30 pm but due to the First Friday mass at 7:00 pm the presentation in church with Fr. Roberto Corral will begin at 7:30 p.m. Come and enjoy!

On next Sunday, March 3rd, at 3:00 pm we are hosting for the first time an Interfaith Contra Costa County concert entitled, "All are One." Six groups, including our Christ the King Youth Band and Singers, will perform and a reception will follow. There is no charge.

I also want to call your attention to the brand new opportunity to explore avenues of social justice which may be open for us. Join us Thursday, March 7th at 7:00pm. This will be your chance to meet other people interested in getting involved in this vital ministry and get connected with people who already are very involved. At this meeting there will be easy opportunities to volunteer.

Remember, I promised you and you may have promised yourself, fifteen minutes of spiritual reading each day during Lent. For the fast readers among you here are two more suggestions: *God Speaks in Many Tongues* by Sr. Joan Chittister and *Simplifying the Soul* by Paula Huston.

All Are Welcome

Bulletin Letter — December 22, 2013

Christmas time is one season of the year when we are reminded we must be a welcome place for everyone. As James Joyce famously said of the Catholic Church, "Here comes everyone." Whatever your reason, history or motivation here at Christ the King, we want you to know you are most welcome.

Another parish, St. Patrick's in Oakland, put it this way:

"We extend a special welcome to those who are single, married, divorced, gay, filthy rich, dirt poor, *yo no hablo ingles.* We extend a special welcome to those who are crying newborns, skinny as a rail, or could afford to lose a few pounds. We welcome you if you can sing like Andrea Bocelli or like our pastor who can't carry a note in a bucket. You're welcome here if you're "just browsing," just woke up or just got out of jail. We don't care if you're more Catholic than the Pope or haven't been in church since little Joey's Baptism. We extend a special welcome to those who are over 60, but not grown up yet, and to teenagers who are growing up too fast. We welcome soccer moms, NASCAR dads, starving artists, tree huggers, latte sippers, vegetarians, junk-food eaters. We welcome those who are in recovery or still addicted. We welcome you if you're having problems or you're down in the dumps, or if you don't like "organized religion," we've been there too. If you blew all your offering money at the dog track, work too hard, don't work, can't spell, or because grandma is in town and wanted to go to church. We welcome those who are inked, pierced or both. We offer a special welcome to those who could use a prayer now, had religion shoved down your throat as a kid or got lost in traffic and wound up here by mistake. We welcome tourists, seekers and doubters, bleeding hearts . . . and you!"

Class Reunion

Homily at 52nd Class Reunion — May 6, 2015
by Fr. Dan Danielson

This is our 52nd year reunion for those of us who were ordained, the 64th for those of us who entered St. Joseph's College in 1951.

It is clear to all of us now, as we gather, that we are in the final stages of life. We're playing on the back nine. We all ache somewhere.

Many of our classmates have already passed on. Our life's work is largely behind us. We are, for the most part, "retired," though that term is open to various interpretations. Those of us who pastored parishes have passed that responsibility on to others. Those of us who raised children, now have passed the responsibilities for the next generation on to them, and we can enjoy the time we have with grandchildren—without the burden of responsibility.

Whatever we have accomplished in the Church or in the world is now passed. Our resume is completed. And we can take a look back and say: "Well done!" "Good effort!"

But we may have deeper questions at this point in life: "What does it all mean, really?" "What gives our life meaning, value, purpose now and from here on out?"

And this is where our Christian faith becomes all important. For God alone gives ultimate meaning to all our activities and accomplishments here on earth. Our faith lets us know that it was all worth it—the sacrifices, the hard times, the hard work, the anxieties, hurts and disappointments that accompany every human life at some point. We know we are flawed creatures but also splendidly endowed. And though we know we are not the center of the universe and are prone to error, mistake and sin, yet we know that we are loved and that ultimately we serve a higher purpose. Because we are joined as branches to the True Vine which gives us strength and life, because we remain one with Him, we have been able to bear much true fruit in this life—and beyond.

The second question in our grammar school catechism, before the Second Vatican Council was: "Why did God make me?" "God made me to know Him, to love Him and to serve Him in this life and to be happy with Him forever in the next." That is the fulfillment of our destiny; that is our lasting hope; that is the source of our abiding joy as we go through the various stages of our diminishment. To be able to accept that "lessening" with peace and tranquility—that is the grace we pray for this day—for all of us.

In the end, all is grace. My overwhelming experience at this stage of life is gratitude. For we are all embraced and accepted. We don't have to struggle for a place. Each of our lives has been organized around a vocation, a call to respond to what life and the Lord has asked of us, even if at times we weren't sure what that vocation was or were unable to articulate it clearly.

We commend to the Lord's mercy all our classmates who have gone home before us, and the deceased professors, confessors, friends and spouses who have guided and helped us along our journeys. And we look forward to gathering one day in an eternal reunion, where our care and love for one another has no bounds and no end.

For the time being, we rejoice that we can be together this day, that we can smile and eat and drink and renew our friendships with each other.

I can see a time when our reunions will be smaller and smaller, ultimately coming down to three old men having dinner, hoisting a drink to the past and going quietly to bed.

There is peace and deep joy in finishing our journey. May the Lord bless us all and enable us to go gently into that "good night." We don't have to "rage against the dying of the light," as Dylan Thomas suggests, because we are rather to be embraced by the everlasting light that will never fade or go dark.

Homily at Brian's Retirement

Homily at Brian's Retirement Mass —
September 14, 2014
by Bishop John Cummins

Introduction by Fr. Brian Joyce:

Now I want to invite a close friend, Bishop John Cummins,
to share with me and share with you. Bishop Cummins . . .

Homily:

In 1963, St. Patrick's Seminary, which was and is the seminary
for the Archdiocese of San Francisco, produced one of its largest
classes for ordination. I would think that most of us would agree
along with the numbers, the corresponding level of talent that
came with that class was extraordinary. Now they have stayed
very close to each other and they have been very loyal. At the
same time, they put together a fierce kind of competitiveness
which I think is part of the reason they were so well-suited as
priests of their generation.

Now, six of those served in the Diocese of Oakland, but
of course, Fr. Brian Joyce was one of them. Now, I would say
well-suited for their time, because along with their talent, and
I give much more credit to this than they do in their seminary
time, but that they were formed in a much wider pattern than
we were. Theological grounding was not very different from,
really, the time or perhaps the time of St. Vincent de Paul in the
1600s. But there were two things that indicated some shift and
some change. And the first was that after looking forward to
serving in the Archdiocese of San Francisco, which would have
placed them anywhere between Stanislaus County, Mendocino
and Santa Clara.

In 1962, their sights had to be changed very radically because the Diocese of Oakland was established. There has been no boundary change for almost 100 years and they would be focused therefore on the two counties. What they did not realize was that the Bishop would be a very distant figure and San Francisco would be very intertwined with their lives in the Diocese of Oakland. Now, the other thing that made the difference, the surprise in 1959 of Pope John the XXIII saying, "We are going to have an Ecumenical Council." Now, all four years that they had theology there really was that light overhanging them, creating an atmosphere of uncertain anticipation that there was going to be change. They had the advantage of two young priests who really helped them and prepared them all that way. And one was **Fr. Frank Norris**, a product of San Francisco, in theology and **Fr. Robert Giguire** in philosophy, who made a great impact on these men as they were developing. Now, as the Council developed these conclusions, I would say that this group of young men were better prepared for the changes that came than the most of us, even though now I say we have imbibed those themes: The Church as the people of God, the universal call to holiness, active liturgical participation through scriptural prayer and reflection, the health of the Church through ministry, and our openness to the world, especially though dialogue that was so highly regarded by Pope Paul VI.

Now, the suitability of Fr. Brian Joyce with that orientation is what we talk about today. Now, I remember within one year of his ordination. I know it was in Berkeley. I knew the room very, very well, but I can't remember what the topic was exactly, but Berkeley was very much into the Ecumenical activities in those days. And in the question-and-answer period this young priest, just ordained, about half way back on the right side, with maybe 80 or 90 people present, got up to add a little correction or refining about . . . . As I say, I can't remember the topic, but I remember when I got home that night and said, "This guy has a mind like a scalpel."

Now, Bishop Begin recognized that very quickly because after a cup of tea at Lawrence O'Toole and a short time at St. Augustine in Oakland, Brian was sent back to Manhattan College in the Bronx. Now, this Oakland native from St. Anthony Parish wasn't the least bit overwhelmed by the big city. He did very well and met the famous people, **Gabriel Moran**, who was very much in tune with the Second Vatican Council, **Harry Brown**, a colorful pastor, who occasionally is a part of our conversation to this day. But he also met **Peter Steinfelds**, and his New Jersey connections came from that same part of the time. When he came home he was Director of Adult Education, a brand new department in the Diocese. Now you in the parish are the recipients of that preparation. Quality of preaching for example, the breadth of adult education that has gone on here. I just would mention **Brian Swimme**, the doctor in cosmology and faith and reason, and Brian and Brian became a traveling tour for faith and reason. The critic and the historian **Gary Wills**, the KQED forum man, **Michael Krasny**, Islamic experts. I'm aware that you even demanded that Brian Joyce give you the story of who are the heroes in his life. But I would say especially the church bulletins every week, and I would use the word again, "scalpel." Topics of Church, topics of the world, topics of immediacy and that they would be pointed, concise and succinct. They really are fit for the archives of the Diocese of Oakland. But well-suited meant the parish as articulated by our Pope Francis, "The parish is capable of self-renewal, constant adaptivity, and continues to be the church living in the midst of the homes of her sons and daughters."

Now, Brian's identification is really parish priest and I commend you for your collaboration with him in so many ways. The hospitality that you have shared with him to those who come here to visit or were new and that hospitality is of course the essential element, really, of a contemporary parish. I also commend you for your ministries with the cohesion that has become because of them. And the blessing of inclusion, not just of those who minister here but in a very special way Msgr. James Wade in his retirement. Now, that is the tradition with Brian Joyce. He was very faithful to his pastor at St. Anthony's at the time he went to the seminary. I think just as well in his living while he was Chancellor with Fr. Gus Quinn. A powerful leader of the priests in this diocese and one who had very traditional credentials, but one who was very important in the changes in the Second Vatican Council. Now, there was one moment I remember, when he was living with Gus Quinn. Gus had a St. Bernard dog, and I don't know how much Brian liked the dogs but the evening that the dog came in and put his jaw on the dining table while they were eating was not well received by Brian Joyce. Now, I would say the spread of ministries in this parish are very significant and that perhaps I might describe them as, "He was in the midst of all of you, but was not in your hair."

Now, **Paul Wilkes**, the American journalist, when he was looking across the country to find vibrant, American parishes included of course, Christ the King, Pleasant Hill. Now, the responsibility of priests goes beyond the parish, and the heritage of Vatican II demands that one raises the sights beyond the local community and that meant, I suppose, first of all the Diocese and Brian was chancellor for the decade of the 70s. He has written his notes about getting along with the old pastor, who was the vicar general and the bishop as well, because I think Brian was not adverse to writing letters in his youth or even commenting about things before then. But I would say beyond that, two stories I just would mention. He was very active with the Council of Priests and a quarter-century ago he persuaded the Council of Priests to develop Diocesan Pastoral Council, laity, religious, clergy around the bishop. Only half our parishes had Pastoral Councils and I was very hesitant about whether the timing was right, but it was very right. And Brian sold that Pastoral Council at two long weekends at Holy Names University setting up what the Council should be and what the priorities should be. And number three was a surprise, social justice. I think that what came out of that was an identification of social justice as mainstream, not just the work of activists but that group picked out inner city schools are the work of justice; St. Vincent de Paul in its rehabilitation of those incarcerated a matter of justice; our Catholic hospitals at that time lobbying for universal healthcare. I remember when Bishop Vigneron came, the first time he met the crowd, I don't know, with surprise but certainly with compliment he said, "This is a very mature group." And the second thing, when we decided we would build a cathedral, Brian ended up in charge of the committee to select an architect. We did not advertise, but we had thirteen architects, really international in character, who applied for the position. Brian worked out a procedure. Those thirteen were reduced to five, then to three, then to one, so that we could get on with the work.

Now, beyond the diocese of course, he received national notice. When the project for parish renewal was created by the American Bishops, centered in New York, he was invited back to be the staff. I appreciated the compliment, but I did not like the position. He was number-two man. He really had the talent for being number-one man. He decided not to go. But the national bishops had from the time of the Vatican Council a committee on priestly life and ministry, and he was tagged to be involved with that, and I approved of that very, very much. He gave council to the directions that committee would take. He wrote a number of the documents or parts of the documents. I think the one that is significant to remember is he wrote the one on *Priests and Stress*. Then, he went around the country promoting that document. And I remember, I think it was when he went to the Archdiocese of Portland, Oregon, he came back and mentioned that perhaps he was exhibit A in one way of the problem of stress. And I do recall he put skiing in the proper order in his life from that time on. As well as the accepting, when he first came to Christ the King, of sitting down every day at lunch with Msgr. James Wade. That was a pattern that was very unfamiliar to Brian before he came to Pleasant Hill.

Now we are in the moment of transition today and we are into, I don't want to say retirement. I do agree very much with the Sister from Berkley who said, "Our time has a new normal, and retirement means something else." I'm sure for example that Brian will maintain the message on his voice mail that's been on there for years, and I've heard it so often, "I'll get back to you so quickly you'll hardly believe it." Now, he is the last of the class of 1963 to lay down the burden of administration. I suppose it was out of some conviction, but I think he loved the work and so adapted to what he was doing. Some suitable words became a little challenge for me, but I thought back to something that they and we in our time. There is some irony about this, because it's done by a British poet, and I'm representing it for the son of the Aran Islands on the West of Ireland, but it is that Homeric poem and the settling down after the wars:

"Though much is taken, much abides and though we are not now that strength which in old days moved earth and heaven, that which we are, we are. One equal temper of heroic hearts made weak by time and fate but strong in will to strive, to seek, to find, not to yield."

Now, my theme about well-suited, I think the title "A Man for All Seasons" is elsewhere claimed. I think sufficient for us on this day is a man of his time and abundantly so, and we have been the beneficiaries.

Fr. Brian Joyce's words after the Bishop spoke:

I want to say a word of sincere thanks to Bishop Barber and to Bishop Cummins for their complimentary words about my life and my ministry and my supposed talents. I'm glad to know that they obviously don't know the half of it. I'm glad you do.

I want you to sit down and relax for a bit. I am going to show a video. Now, most of you have seen much of this video already but the music is different, some of the pictures are different. I want to include my dancing career in it, because some of you saw it last week and you didn't know I was dancing with fourteen other priests, and we want to see who all those priests are. I am delighted my classmates are here and delighted with what John said about our class. Absolutely true. Outstanding lights including **Tony Valdivia, Dan Danielson, Dan Derry**, who was at the altar with me, and the brightest light of our class can't be with us today, **Don Osuna**. My most striking memory of Don was in the 1960s at the funeral of Msgr. Pinkie O'Donnell, who was the founding pastor of the Oakland Cathedral. For the responsorial at his request and the request of his dear friend, Msgr. Charlie Hackel, Don sang *I Did It My Way*. We remember today, I was not able to get a hold of Don, so I got a second rate backup by the name of Elvis. Let's sit back and enjoy.

AFTERWORD

As a recently retired priest, I have been able to travel extensively and to reflect considerably on the faith and practices of Catholics today. My central question remains to ask what are the characteristics of what we once called "practicing Catholics"? Once upon a time, the answer was clear, concise and completely agreed upon. When I was growing up, earlier in the last century, the definition of "practicing Catholics" was more than obvious. Very simply it meant someone who: 1) went to Mass on Sunday; 2) abstained from meat on Friday; and, 3) went to confession with some regularity. My memory is that in those days confession was presented as absolutely necessary and that we needed it frequently.

Much to my surprise, and quite frankly my delight, when you ask knowledgeable Catholics today what defines "practicing Catholics," whether they are old China hands, such as the experienced Maryknoll priests I met with and discussed with in Hong Kong, or more recent and modern Catholics, whom I met with at the Call to Action Convention in Memphis, Tennessee, or those I met with in the School of the Americas Protest in Fort Benning, Georgia, or the elderly but quite modern Catholics I was arrested with on the past Good Friday at Lawrence Livermore Laboratory in California, they simply either do not know or clearly there is no consensus. I find this to be appropriate and delightful, because as Catholics today we are not called to one simple formula or set of behaviors. Rather, we are called to holiness and to the challenge to be simply the best we are.

"Practicing Catholics" are not what is thought of as either typical Catholics or core Catholics, but somewhere in between. As a recent American magazine described them, "typical Catholics" (45%) go to Church once a month and on major holidays while "core Catholics" (4%) attend Masses weekly and make other Church activities happen. What we knew and loved as "practicing Catholics" ends up somewhere in between, neither attending daily Mass nor abstaining from weekly Mass.

Again, I want to ask, what are the characteristics of "practicing Catholics" today? Frankly, I am at heart such a pre-Vatican II Catholic that, even now, I search for three simple criteria or answers, when I search for a practicing Catholic. What do you thank the three would be?

In my estimation the first is clear and simple. It has to do with the Mass and Eucharist, and it calls to mind the early persecuted Catholics in North Africa, who to their judges simply said, "Without the Eucharist, we cannot live." It also has to do with a style of devotion to the Eucharist which Meister Eckhart described in the 13th century by teaching, "If the only prayer you say in your whole life is 'thank you,' that would suffice." Meister Eckhart, like countless Catholics before and after him, believed prayer is primarily an act not of begging or beseeching or wanting or needing, but of thanking. The word *eucharist* comes from the Greek word for "to give thanks." So, Christian worship is primarily a thank-you gathering. Thomas Aquinas also taught that the very essence of true religion is gratitude. How else to explain the very Catholic practice of daily Mass, although admittedly not necessarily valued by "practicing Catholics."

My second and third criteria are less clear and frankly quite surprising. One comes from comments by Kerry Kennedy, the daughter of Bobby Kennedy and niece of John F. Kennedy, who suggested an answer last fall at the Call to Action Conference in Memphis, Tennessee. Another criteria comes from an equally significant person, although quite frankly something of a surprise, and that is our retired Pope Benedict XVI (Ratzinger).

For me the second criteria of active, practicing Catholics today is quite simply that they are concerned enough and committed enough as Catholics to be angry. Whether it is recent church leadership that downplays the teaching of Vatican Council II and the recognition of all of us to be called to holiness or the challenge to be consulted and involved as a people of God. "Practicing Catholics" today are uniformly angry and upset, when they find no trace of consultation. I can recall years ago pointing out that very often the difference between a good Catholic and an active non-Catholic is that the Catholic regularly gets upset at church leadership and teaching, whereas the non-Catholic simply does not care one way or the other.

My third criteria for "practicing Catholics" comes from the comment of Pope Benedict XVI, who clearly states that one of the pillars of Catholicism is a quest for truth. What that means in the practical life of active Catholics today is that they are the ones asking questions, not to attack or criticize, but to search the meaning of our beliefs for our daily lives.

There you have it, my criteria for "practicing Catholics" are: 1) the **Eucharist**, not only attendance but celebration of thanksgiving as central to our daily lives; 2) **Anger**, or at least upset in the sense of caring enough about our Catholic tradition, to change in some way, when we feel it is being betrayed even by the Church itself; and, 3) **Questions**, not so much to attack but to search out our treasures, so we can deeply appreciate and live by them.

The question I end up leaving for myself and everyone else is, are you, or am I, a "practicing Catholic"?

CPSIA information can be obtained at www.ICGtesting.com
Printed in the USA
BVOW11*0217070116

432083BV00008B/22/P